1. **DOWNLOAD** the Must Eat New York app on your iPhone **FOR FREE** from the App Store. Scan the QR code to download the app immediately.

2. Go to **www.musteatnyc.com** and receive a unique activation code for the app. Following activation, your app will receive all the addresses from the book, including all the practical information and numerous extras. See which addresses are close by, search for addresses based on the type of kitchen, add addresses to your favorites, find out how to get there...

MUST
EAT
NYC

MUST EAT

AN ECLECTIC SELECTION
OF CULINARY LOCATIONS

LUC HOORNAERT
PHOTOGRAPHY: KRIS VLEGELS

LANNOO

Scenes from the Battleship Gastronomica in NYC

"What's the purpose of your visit to NYC, sir?" asked the customs officer, minutes after I disembarked at JFK. "Um, well, lunch and dinner," I replied hesitantly. Three minutes later two custom officers were unpacking my luggage with the most sincere interest. I just barely avoided a full body cavity search. But I was telling the truth. I hadn't come to NYC to see the numerous mind-blowing landmarks, the fabulous museums or Broadway shows. I came here to eat, full stop, to give myself over to absolute gastronomical pleasure in all its forms.

As a child of the Old World, it seemed (for a long time) as if I were strapped to some sort of gastronomical chastity belt. Somehow it felt like my taste buds were not allowed to go all the way. My first eating experiences in NYC, however, completely liberated me from the burden of gastronomical history and even "proper gastronomy" which always seemed to peep over my shoulder like a black raven. Entertainment seems to be the hardest word to stomach in the Old World. Here I really found the best of both worlds. Old World focus, depth, and precision, coupled with a New World perspective, playfulness and vision. All of this was 30-odd years ago.

Being a full time importer of wine and high-end Japanese ingredients (in Belgium) gets me around the globe. Wherever I am I always try to scratch the surface to connect with the soul of local gastronomy and eating establishments. Nowhere else have I found more culinary bliss than in NYC.

Must Eat NYC is absolutely not a complete guide; the mere idea that a guide to NYC restaurants could ever be "complete" is utterly preposterous. The NYC food scene is a bit like a Borgesian encyclopedia; unimaginably endless and profoundly strange. *Must Eat NYC* highlights my personal favorites and features those dishes that touch me, embrace me, and make me feel like coming home.

I hope you enjoy and savor this guide as much as I did in its creation.

Luc Hoornaert and Kris Vlegels

Thanks, dear Qurratul-ain, for your patience and strength.
You are the wind beneath my wings.

In aeterna gratitudine to Randall Grahm.

CONTENTS

UPTOWN WEST
Bronx
Manhattan
UPTOWN EAST
MIDTOWN WEST
Queens
MIDTOWN EAST
DOWNTOWN WEST / DOWNTOWN EAST
Brooklyn
Staten Island

SMORGASBURG

East River State Park (Kent Ave. & N. 7th St.), Williamsburg, Waterfront
Open Sat: 11:00 a.m. - 6:00 p.m.
Brooklyn Bridge Park Pier 5, Williamsburg, Brooklyn
Open Sun: 11:00 a.m. - 6:00 p.m.

Every time I walk the streets of NYC after a harsh winter and here
and there espy Japanese cherry blossoms announcing the tide of spring, I cry with joy.
It is Smorgasburg time again!

Local vendors

Smorgasburg is an initiative of Brooklyn Flea, a company that specializes in organizing large flea markets throughout the entire east coast of the US. Because more and more food stands joined and offered their services, they decided that it was time for a new initiative. Smorgasburg (a combination of Smorgasbord and Williamsburg) is one of the biggest weekly food events in the US.

More than one hundred food stands offer their specialties at this Woodstock for food lovers. Some stands are very modest, while others come out ablaze in visual spectacle. Just as NYC is a cultural melting pot, so is this NYC version of the famous Jamaa-el-Fnaa in Marrakesh – a real gastronomical melting pot.

At times only the breathtaking view of the Manhattan skyline and the Brooklyn Bridge betray the fact that you are not in some exotic *souk*, but in Brooklyn. Every time I am set loose here, I reach my limit... and want more! And that is perfectly permissible, because anyone who can resist is not a real foodie.

EXCELL'S KINGSTON EATERY

90 Kent Avenue, Brooklyn - NY 11211
T (917) 244-1046 - www.excelleatery.com
Open Sat-Sun: 11:00 a.m. - 6:00 p.m.

Excell's Kingston Eatery is a catering business in Brooklyn that specializes in dishes from its owners' native Jamaica.

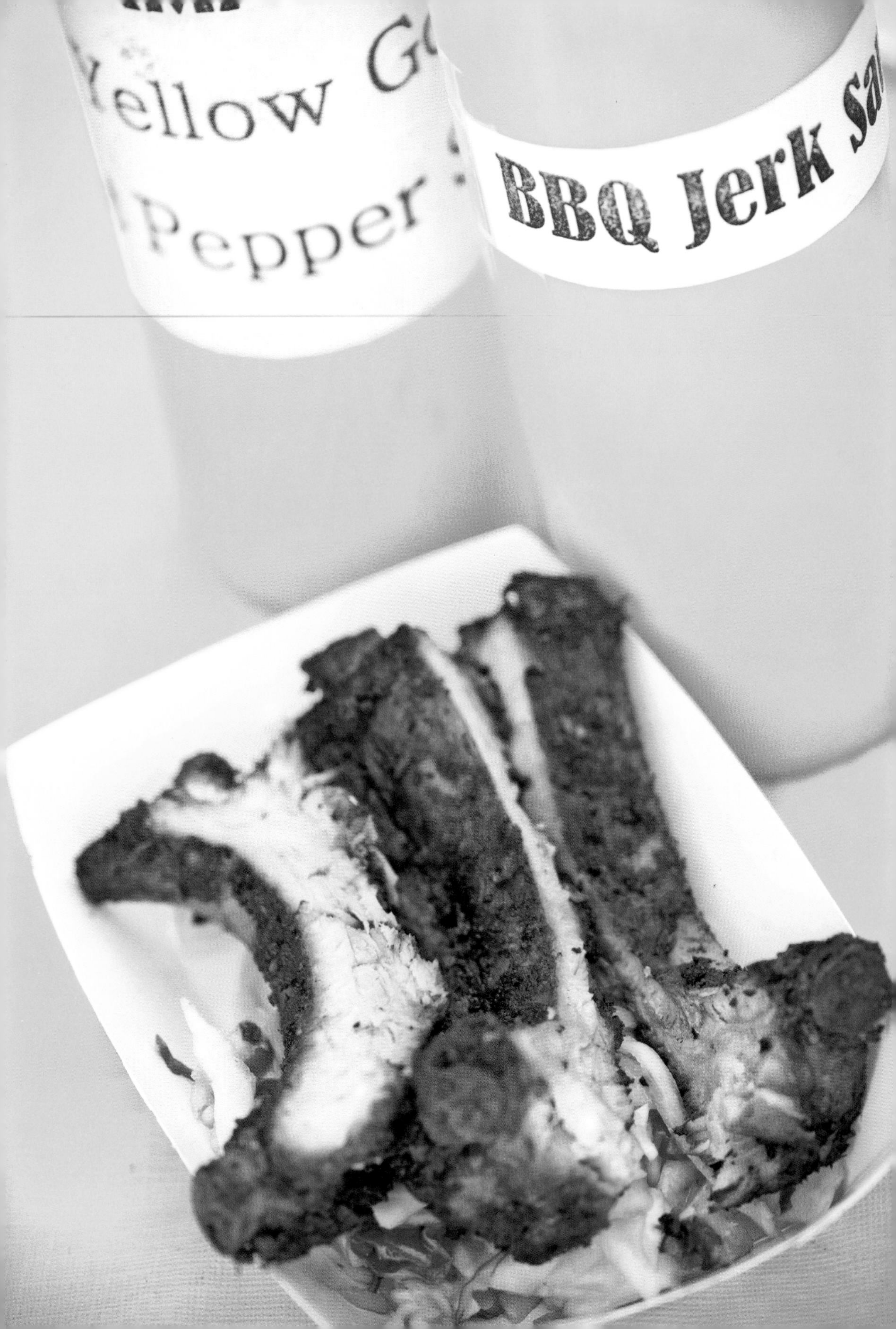
Yellow
Pepper
BBQ Jerk

not only in Jamaica!

Jerk chicken, Festival, Yordie slaw & fried plantains

Smorgasburg is the ideal location for them to acquaint New Yorkers with their less familiar cuisine.

Jerk is a preparation method that you find in the Caribbean, especially in Jamaica. The meat, usually chicken or pork, is dry-rubbed with pimento, Scotch Bonnet peppers and a dry mixture of nutmeg, scallions, garlic, thyme, salt and cloves. The meat is then dry-baked, traditionally in a pit fire. The term comes from the Spanish charqui, which was corrupted in English and became "jerky." The origin of jerk is most likely African and stems from an obscure past. The area that is now Ghana was the land of the Akan people, who lived along the coast. This population was a popular target for slave hunters and its people were brought by the Spanish colonists to the Carib-bean, and therefore also to Jamaica. When the British invaded Jamaica in 1655, the Spanish colonists fled and their Coromantee slaves – from the Gold Coast of Ghana – escaped into Jamaica's mountainous regions where they integrated with the local Taínos.

The subtle balance and the delicate seasoning reveal the true taste of Jamaica in this jerk chicken. The chicken looks quite impressive in virtue of its dark color and tastes intensively of its well-balanced spice mixture. Another Jamaican specialty that naturally accompanies the chicken is Festival, which is actually fried beignets made from flour, corn flour, water, yeast, salt and of course a bit of vanilla. Add to this fried green bananas, a helping of crunchy lettuce and you have a feast.

BOLIVIAN LLAMA PARTY

27 North 6th St. - NY 11211
T (347) 395 5481 - www.facebook.com/Bolivianllamaparty/info
Open Sat-Sun: 11:00 a.m. - 6:00 p.m.

Patrick and David Oropeza are two proud Bolivians.
Their pride is so great that they established a take-out restaurant in Brooklyn
in order to make the tasty Bolivian kitchen more accessible to people.

Beef brisket chola

this 10-ingredient sandwich
is a real taste sensation

Apparently, Bolivian cuisine does not particularly excel in exporting itself, because I can't think of a single Bolivian restaurant. Nevertheless, the taste of a well-run Bolivian kitchen is fascinating. The deep roots of the cuisine go back to the Aymara civilization, a population group that lived in the Andes and Altiplano. The Aymaras were first conquered by the Incas in the 15th century and later by the Spaniards. After the Spanish American War (1810-1825), the Aymara people were divided between two new states: Bolivia and Peru. With deep roots of Spanish influence, the only dish with a bit of international recognition was the salteña, better known as empanada.

Either way, the Bolivian Beef Brisket chola is a bombardment of flavors to your taste buds; the combination of vivid flavors is superb. There are ten ingredients: the base is slow-cooked beef brisket dry-rubbed with ten spices and the definitive presence of fennel seeds and smoked garlic, on top of that homemade cheese, huacatay aïoli (with the typical taste of tarragon and marigold) salsa criolla, ali panka, home-preserved carrots, red onion with hibiscus and homemade chili marinated in chicha. Just a bite of this and you ask yourself why there are no Bolivian restaurants in the San Pellegrino Top 50. To get such a taste sensation from a sandwich is truly exceptional.

PARANTHA ALLEY

East River State Park (Kent Avenue & N. 7 Street) - Williamsburg, Waterfront
sat 11.00 a.m. - 18.00 p.m.
Tobacco Warehouse 28 Water Street, Dumbo
Sun 11.00 a.m. - 18.00 p.m.

The Vedas are the general name for the very ancient scriptures that form the basis
for the Upanishads, the foundation of Indian philosophy
and of many religions connected to Hinduism.

Qeema paratha

especially in North INdia the paratha is insanely popular

In these scriptures, which were written between 1500 and 1000 BCE, one already finds mention of the paratha. At that time, paratha (or parantha) was an important part of the daily diet of the population. The actual word paratha comes from the Veda's Sanskrit where the purodashas were offered to the fire gods during very specific ceremonies. These were always filled with lentil powder and finely chopped vegetables.

Currently, paratha is an essential part of breakfast in large parts of northern Asia. It is a flat bread that looks more like a pancake. Since paratha is also an amalgam of parat and atta, together meaning layers of dough, the concoction becomes immediately clear. Dough, water and ghee, that's all you need. The fresh, rolled-out dough balls are baked on a hot tava. In north India especially, the paratha is insanely popular.

Parantha Alley is not only the name of this unique food stall, but it is also the name of a street in the old quarters of Delhi, a street known for its paratha makers. The gali paranthe wali (literally: the lane of those who bake bread) is the name of a narrow street in the Chandni Chowk neighborhood of Delhi. These days there are only a few paratha makers in this street, which was built under the famous Shah Jahan.

When you stand in front of this wonderful food stall on Smorgasburg and the fresh paratha dough balls are rolled out and baked with lots of ghee, you know that for only a few dollars you get the most delicious taste explosion on your plate and lots of history for free. Your choice of filling is rolled into the paratha dough and then baked. You also get all sorts of homemade side dishes, sauces and dips alongside. I usually go for the coriander chutney, roasted chili, lightly pickled preserved mango, marinated onions and a bit of refreshing cucumber raita.

GRIMALDI'S

1 Front St., Brooklyn - NY 11201
T (718) 858-4300 - www.grimaldis.com
Open Mon-Thurs: 11:30 a.m. - 10:45 p.m., Fri: 11:30 a.m. -11:45 p.m., Sat: noon - 11:45 p.m., Sun: noon - 10:45 p.m.

Under the Brooklyn Bridge, of course on the Brooklyn side, you will always see a long line of people waiting in front of a very handsome building. These are the pizza enthusiasts waiting for a table at Grimaldi's, one of NY's best-loved pizzerias.

Pizza Margherita

You can't reserve a table here and nope, they don't accept credit cards either.

One of the darkest days in Italian culinary history must have been when someone placed pineapple (from a can) for the first time on a pizza base and stuck it in the oven. Yet pizza Hawaii is the most popular pizza in Italy, thanks of course to the tourists. Pizza originated in the Mediterranean Sea area and people surmise that it began as a plate! In other words, people baked flat bread that was used as a tray. Everything that people wanted to eat was laid on it and only if one had an extremely big appetite, the 'plate' was also devoured. According to tradition, the Trojan hero Aeneas established the city of Lavinium on the spot where he devoured the empty plates (bread plates) himself out of hunger.

The Vikings also ate a type of pizza, namely a round-shaped bread with all sorts of ingredients on it which was baked in a type of pizza oven. It was only in the 17th century that pizza made its appearance in Naples, without the tomato sauce of course because at that time tomatoes were (erroneously) considered toxic. Tomatoes from South America were introduced in Europe around 1500 and were mostly a yellow variety. That is why the Italian name for tomato is pomo d'oro, which means "golden apple". The tomatoes that we see today were developed by means of cross-fertilization in the 18th century.

The best-known pizza in those days was the Mastunicola, a pizza base decked with lard, pecorino, black pepper and basil.

Most people still consider pizza Margherita *the* most authentic pizza. It was created by Raffaele Esposito, one of the best-known pizza makers in Naples. He had the honor of making a pizza for King Umberto I and his wife Margherita. His chauvinism inspired him to create a pizza with the colors of the Italian flag (tomato sauce, buffalo mozzarella and basil) and that's how pizza Margherita was born.

In 1941, when Patsy Grimaldi was just ten years old, he lived in the Italian part of Harlem where he learned the skills of pizza making. Patsy dreamed of having his own pizza restaurant in Manhattan, but there was one problem: You can only achieve the wonderful thin and crispy bottom and crust in an oven that ideally reaches a temperature of approximately 932° F. That is only possible in an oven fueled by charcoal or coal. His dream was shattered because Manhattan didn't permit new construction of such ovens. But in Brooklyn that was still possible, and so the location was moved to the current address! The oven weighs 25 tons and runs at a toasty but comfortable temperature of approximately 1202° F. (still pretty damn hot). Fresh dough, a daily delivery of super-fresh mozzarella and fresh San Marzano tomatoes do the rest.

SUNDAY, JUNE 1ST

SAKE KASU CHALLAH, RAISIN BUTTER - 7
WEAKFISH SASHIMI SALAD - 15
SMOKED TORO TOASTS, RAMP CREAM CHEESE - 9
SPRING JEW EGG - 13
CHILLED CHAWANMUSHI, HONSHIMEJI, SPRING ONIONS, SHRIMP - 14
UNA TATAKI, BLACK TAHINI - 17
ABURAAGE POUCHES, RACLETTE, GREEN TOMATO RELISH - 10
OKONOMIYAKI, CORNED LAMB'S TONGUE, BONITO - 11
AGE DASHI TOFU, FAVAS, GREEN BEANS, FRESH CHICKPEAS - 13
TERIYAKI DUCK WINGS - 15
MATZO BALL RAMEN - 17
SASHA-CRUSTED FLUKE, ASPARAGUS, MUSHROOMS, SAKE BEURRE BLANC - 26
PASTRAMI-STUFFED CHICKEN, CABBAGE, POTATO SALAD - 27
GYU STEAK, EGGPLANT AKA MISO, TOKYO TURNIP, RICE CAKE - 32
LOX BOWL, RICE, DAIKON, AVOCADO, IKURA - 23

SHALOM JAPAN

310 S 4th St. (@Rodney Street) - NY 11211
T (718) 388-4012 - www.shalomjapannyc.com
Open Tues-Wed: 6:00 p.m. -10:00 p.m., Fri-Sat: 6:00 p.m. -11:00 p.m., Sun: 6:00 p.m. - 10:00 p.m., Sat-Sun: brunch 11:00 a.m. - 3:00 p.m.

Sawako Okochi and Aaron Israel, both chefs at Shalom Japan, are gastronomical jacks-of-all-trades and that has a lot to do with their cultural origins. Sawako, born in Hiroshima, came to NYC in 2000 via Texas. Aaron, who grew up in Great Neck, has worked in some of the most acclaimed culinary establishments.

Okonomiyaki, salt-cured lamb's tongue, bonito flakes

Together, they are not only a couple, but also Shalom Japan, a most unusual name for a restaurant. The name, by the way, came from a kosher restaurant on 22 Wooster Street in Soho, where Miriam Mizakura, a Japanese Jewess sang, danced and cracked Jewish jokes. She served gefilte sashimi and challah singing *Hava Nagila*. Unfortunately this restaurant stopped existing some 10 odd years ago.

It is easy to find. A few blocks from the Williamsburg Bridge, you follow the sounds of hip-hop music typically coming from the youngsters playing basketball on the court in the Rodney Park Playground and it is directly on the other side.

This restaurant is more than a unique collaboration; it is actually the melting together of two separate cultures, cooking experiences and a passion for fine food. This has resulted in mature, but playful dishes that show great respect for both cultures. At first glance, the Jewish gastronomic culture does not seem to share the same level of refinement as the supremely refined Japanese food culture, but somehow the collaboration works brilliantly. A major advantage in making this work is the immense selection of fresh and dry products available in this city.

Making a food choice is my most difficult task in this restaurant, because as a Japanese food freak, I am naturally very curious about what I get in a fusion with the Jewish kitchen. Their version of one of my favorite lunch dishes in Japan, okonomiyaki, is indeed very successful and perhaps an improvement of the original. With the addition of a nearly candied lamb's tongue, I enjoyed the essential, full texture that you get in okonomiyaki.

Okonomiyaki is a popular lunch dish in the Land of the Rising Sun. It might be described as somewhere between a pancake and a hearty omelet filled with leek, Chinese cabbage and delicious nagaimo (yams); it is all topped with Japanese mayonnaise and otafuku sauce (a sort of sweet Japanse Worcestershire), and on top of that, you'll find a bit of grated hana katsuo and ginger. This fast, delicious and sexy lunch is glorious and shows a lesser known aspect of the very diverse Japanese kitchen.

As a huge fan of black sesame and tuna, I was very impressed by the tuna tataki with black tahini. Lovely, barely cooked tuna in a circle of black tahini is once again a very smart fusion. Black sesame is actually used a lot in Japanese desserts and this dish is an upscale version of the nearly classical black sesame-crusted tuna.

When you go out, take a good look at the Star of David and the Rising Sun that flow into each other. For me, this is one of the few establishments that actually understands the meaning of fusion cooking.

TRAIF

229 S 4th St. (between Havemeyer and Roebling St.) - NY 11211
T (347) 844-9578 - www.traifny.com
Open Fri-Sat: 6:00 p.m. -1:00 a.m., Tues -Thurs and Sun: 6:00 p.m. - midnight

On the way to Traif I asked directions from one of the many Chassidic Jews walking
on Havemeyer. My best Yiddish (which sounds not utterly dissimilar from Flemish)
was almost adequate, but then I realized that traif is the Yiddish word for non-kosher food,
which is forbidden according to strict Jewish dietary laws.

A celebration of pork

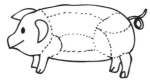

When I arrived, I noticed that the small, delicate logo on the door pictured a cute little piglet with a very small heart. I find this to be very subtle humor for this neighborhood and even more so because one of the couple/owners, Jason Marcus and Heather Heuser... is Jewish. (This is in, fact, the only way they can pull off this caper.)

Jason is not just any cook; Le Bernardin and Eleven Madison Park stand out on his CV. This philosopher, by the way, stands alongside his cooks, working in the tiny kitchen. The menu is very much tied to the season and therefore it constantly changes. The concept here is to order small and big dishes that you can share with other people at your table.

I think that Jason has been rather underrated as a chef (maybe it's the cuteness of the concept), and consequently, Traif is a rather underrated restaurant. Every meal I have enjoyed in Traif was a direct hit! His ability to combine flavors is a refined development. If I see how busy the place is, then I know that by now a lot people have discovered Jason's fantastic dishes.

Jason and Heather met while working together in a restaurant in San Diego. When they fell in love, they set out on a clear course: travel through Europe, go live in NY and then open a restaurant called Traif. In Barcelona they had sat at a bar called Xix (pronounced "chicks" in Catalan). Sometime later, when they had already established Traif, premises down the street (at 241 4th St.) became available. They thought back to their experience at Xix, and voilà, Xixa was conceived. Their new establishment was designed in a cool and esthetic manner and Xixa (pronounced "shiksa" in Spanish) is a playful reference to the cozy bar in Barcelona and to the fact that Heather is Jason's "shiksa", which in Yiddish means a non-Jewish woman (typically a girlfriend). Xixa, nominally a "Mexican" restaurant, can be thought of as a bit like a transposition of Traif to Mexico City. Xixa has an unbelievably good vibe and atmosphere plus the extra touch of cocktails and an impressive wine list. I am an absolute fan of Jason's kitchen and of Heather's sense for detail and service. (And their wicked sense of humor.) A top combination.

ROBERTA'S

261 Moore St. (between Bogart and White St.) - NY 11206
T (718) 417-1118 - www.robertaspizza.com
Open Mon-Fri: 11:00 a.m. - midnight, Sat-Sun: 10:00 a.m. - midnight

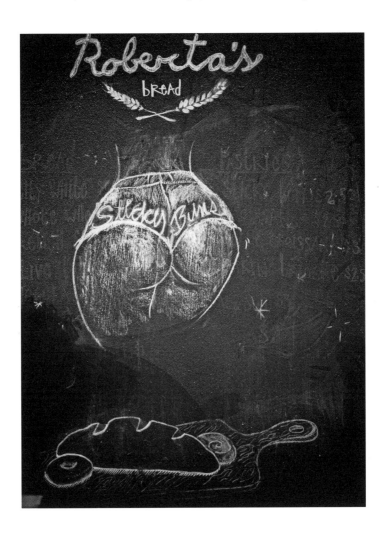

If you walk into a restaurant and see containers with Evergreen printed on them, a radio studio 'on the air' next to someone who is sitting to eat, a drawing of a scantily covered woman's buttocks that says Nice Buns, Mexican Christmas lights, a fire-spitting pizza oven, an ode to cowboys in love from *Brokeback Mountain* (drawn as a pizza face), and you hear *Master of Puppets* banging from the loud speakers, then you are probably sitting at Roberta's.

The Cowabunga Dude pizza

the Mad MAx version of the traditional American diner

On a desolate street in Bushwick, you will find this Mad Max version of a classical American diner. It is a bit of a hipster utopia, but Roberta's means mainly fun, entertainment and damn good food. I absolutely do not want to reduce this restaurant to a pizzeria, but half the guests here eat pizza because it is really awesome. Perfect control of the dough mixture, dripping with mozzarella, does the trick according to Lauren Calhoun, the "pizza boss". The pizza toppings change constantly. I was a fan of their breakfast burrito pizza and of the Cheezus Christ, but right now, I am in my Cowabunga Dude pizza period: tomato, caciocavallo, pepperoni, mushrooms, onions, green peppers and olives. A real stunner.

I love coming to this place; there is always something to experience, and I repeat – the food is fantastically delicious. To their credit is the homemade duck ham and pastrami sandwich, and if tartare is suggested, nothing can hold me back. All the artisanship and skill come from chef Carlo Mirarchi, a thoroughbred chef who also runs Blanca, the star joint next door. Roberta's is top by all standards.

PETER LUGER

178 Broadway (@Driggs) - NY 11211
T (718) 387-7400 - www.peterluger.com
Open Mon-Thurs: 11:30 a.m. - 9:30 p.m., Fri-Sat: 11:30 a.m. - 10:30 p.m., Sun: 12:30 p.m. - 9:30 p.m.

Some restaurants – fortunately, for the most part – have a Zagat Award hanging
high in a place of honor. When you open the door to this establishment,
you see thirty Zagat Awards lined up in three rows of ten.

Steak for two, creamed spinach, German baked potatoes, steaksauce

Yessiree, for thirty consecutive years, Peter Luger has been chosen as the best steakhouse in NYC by the most influential culinary guides in the US. And if you take a moment to look around the place and see the long wooden bar, the candlesticks and the simple tables, you can be sure of one thing: the awards are not for the decor!

Stepping in is also going back a bit in history. In 1887, Carl Luger opened here his Café Billiards & Bowling Alley. A few years later, in December 1903, the neighborhood fell under the shadow of the new Williamsburg Bridge and the local population was predominately German. Williamsburg was also suddenly more accessible and business got a boost. Peter Luger (1866-1941) was the owner and his nephew Carl was the chef. Already then, they made a name for themselves with the quality of their beef. In 1950, Peter's son decided to sell the restaurant in a public auction. Bad idea, because by then the neighborhood was populated by Chassidic Jews who had absolutely no interest in their rare beef and especially not in their German background. One of their best customers, Sol Forman, bought the building and business for $35,000. Forman had been taking his customers to eat at Peter Luger for 25 years and he was not about to change this cherished habit. So he simply bought the place and restored it to its glory. For sixty years of his life, Sol had been eating steak at Peter Luger five times per week and died at the age of 98 a happy man.

I cannot and will not reveal the secret of the quality of this place. It begins with the meat that has always been selected according to texture and taste, and is always USDA prime. Moreover, they have become masters in the skill of letting the meat ripen slowly by a dry-ageing method. Thirty years ago I ate here for the first time and already my then inexperienced taste buds told me that this is the place to experience something exceptionally delicious. A meal in this restaurant remains one the things I most look forward to whenever I am back in NYC. The perfect cooked steak, soft as butter yet tasteful, the unbelievably creamy and delicious spinach and the perfect baked potatoes, just like my grandmother used to make. Add a few generous spoonfuls of the unrivaled Peter Luger steak sauce, of which I always buy a few bottles to take home.

In Europe I find that La Table du Boucher in Mons is by far the best steakhouse on our continent. Luc Broutard, whom I call the cow whisperer, is the man who has awakened the entire European continent to beef cattle breeds, ageing and cooking techniques. My G-rated wet dream is to one day eat a Peter Luger USDA prime beef and a Holstein from Luc in the same meal. That for me would be heaven on earth...

GLASSERIE

eat / drink

GLASSERIE

95 Commercial St. (between Box and Ash St.) - NY 11222
T (718) 389-0640 - www.glasserienyc.com
Mon-Thurs: 5:30 p.m. - 11:00 p.m., Fri: 5:30 p.m. - midnight, Sat: 10:00 a.m. - midnight, Sun: 10:00 a.m. - 11:00 p.m.

"Commercial Street?" the taxi driver asks me. "At Box Street?
There is nothing there," he says, "only a few construction sites".

Yellow-fin crudo, strawberries, rhubarb, rose, jalapeno-oil

This dish illustrates the delicateness and subtlety of their cuisine.

Indeed, there are several large construction projects out there to create plenty of living accommodation in Greenpoint, the northern end of Brooklyn.

And indeed, the only taxis that come out here are the ones that drop people off at Glasserie, located in the impressive, former headquarters of Greenpoint Glass Works. This imposing building was built by Christian Dorflinger, a French immigrant from Alsace.

Glasserie belongs to the category of restaurants where you step in and everything seems to fall into place. Owner Sarah Conklin, who is half-Lebanese and grew up in the Middle East, wants her restaurant's kitchen to clearly express her roots and personal preferences.

You don't have to be a bec fin to know how good the food is in this joint. The chef is Eldad Shem Tov, an Israeli whose entire career has been spent with the refined kitchens of the Levant. These influences are clearly there, but in no way domineering. On the contrary, they raise you up into a cloud of flavors; his dishes seem as if they are perfumed by the Middle East, so subtle and fine in flavor they are. The first time I came here, I was totally blown away by the rabbit dish with chickpeas, served with preserved vegetables and a herb salad. This glorious dish of legs of rabbit, confected in duck lard with a slightly smoked flavor, was truly memorable. The saddle was super tender and had the irresistible taste of hawayij, the typical and intense Yemenite spice mix containing ground caraway, saffron, dried onions, cardamom, coriander, black pepper, anise, fennel and ginger, imparting a very characteristic flavor. In the preparation of the other rabbit parts, I thought I also detected urfa biber, which evokes a wonderful smell of sweet plums.

The yellow-fin crudo dish illustrates the delicateness and subtlety of Glasserie's kitchen. Top yellow-fin tuna with strawberries, a hint of rose, refreshing bitter rhubarb, jalapeno oil and, I thought, a whiff of Aleppo pepper. Everything seems to go so naturally here. Sarah Conklin can rest assured that this place is a NY culinary concept in the making.

DIRCK THE NORSEMAN

7 N. 15th St. (between Gem and Franklin St.) - NY 11222
T (718) 389 2940 - www.dirckthenorseman.com
Mon-Thurs: 5:00 p.m. - midnight, Fri: 5:00 p.m. - 2:00 a.m., Sat-Sun: Noon - 2:00 a.m.

One of the first people to settle in Greenpoint
was Dirck Volckertsen.

Braised pig's knuckle

The piece of land now called Brooklyn and of which Greenpoint is a part, was purchased by the Dutch East India Company (VOC) in 1638. In 1645, Dirck Volkertsen, originally from Scandinavia, received the company's blessing to live there and since he came from the far north, he was called Dirk de Noorman, later changed by the British to Dirck the Norseman. He was a ship builder.

Edward Raven is the owner and driving force of the Lane Brewery on Greenpoint Avenue, Brooklyn's most applauded beer store and café where selected beers were poured. A wild plan became a reality in the former plastic factory close to the East River waterfront. The space is very impressive and dominated by a big shiny brewery, which is clearly visible through a large window from every corner of the entire establishment. This place is commanded by brewery and beer phenomenon, Chris Prout. Together, they are Dirck the Norseman, the first real brew pub in Brooklyn. The result is a wonderful, gigantic pub with room for live bands and the immense brewing talent of Chris, who can let loose his full creative talent under the name of Greenpoint Beer & Ale Co.

The food is ingenious and hearty, and attuned to Chris's beers, not an easy feat. That's why the management decided to keep the food simple but tasty. And as everyone knows – simple is not always easy. There are the perfect ribs, the nostalgic-tasting pork shank and the impressive breast of veal – smoked for eleven hours. Wonderful food that goes perfectly with Chris' assertive beers, such as the Tupelo IPA with a touch of honey added to it, yet remaining refreshing and dry, and Helles Gate Smoked Lager, with a subtle smoky taste. Here you can drink sixteen different beers from the tap, ten of which are brewed on site. Dirck the Norseman is a fantastic bistro by all standards; hanging around here is more of a rule than an exception.

FETTE SAU

354 Metropolitan Ave. (between N 4th and Roebling St.) - NY 11211
T (718) 963-3404 - www.fettesaubbq.com
Mon-Thurs: 5:00 p.m. - 11:00 p.m., Fri-Sun: Noon - 11:00 p.m.

Williamsburg is a trendy neighborhood where hobos and graffiti have to compete with gourmet cheese stores, extravagant music happenings, topnotch trendy retail stores and superior restaurants. Some parts of this area actually remind me a bit of Berlin.

Smoked beef brisket, hand-pulled Berkshire pork, housemade Berkshire sausage

From the sidewalk, it is not so easy to spot Fette Sau, but fortunately there is one way of recognizing it, which you cannot miss – the oh-so-wonderful smoky smell of barbecue that seems to linger outside its gate, which sports a tiny, discreet signboard, and entices you inside. You would never suspect that one of NYC's finest barbecue restaurants is located here.

The building that accommodates Fette Sau was previously a garage and in terms of the infrastructure, it still looks like one. A long driveway where simple picnic tables stand leads to the restaurant. The restaurant is a real feast, even before you have had your first bite. The delicious smell that hangs in the air whets your appetite. They use red and white oak, apple, cherry, peach and maple wood to achieve the complex aromas that penetrate the meat. All the wood, by the way, comes from upstate New York. Although Fette Brau – a beer brewed in the Pilsner style especially for them – flows abundantly from the taps, the handgrips of which are old butcher knives, and there is no need for an apéritif due to these delicious aromas. My mouth is watering already.

Beer, by the way, is the strong point of Fette Sau, but that will surprise no one because the owners, Joe Carroll and Kim Barbour, have one of the best beer bars in NYC just on the other side of the street - the Spuyten Duyvil. Belgian beers and obscure mini-breweries are the specialty here. Spuyten Duyvil is a neighborhood in the Bronx, close to Spuyten Duyvil Creek, where the Hudson runs as wild as a spewing devil. History even tells us of a certain Anthony van Corlaer who in 1642 wanted to swim across the Hudson River from Spuyten Duyvil in order to prove there were no devils in the water. Witnesses claimed to have seen a giant fish that grabbed him by the legs and pulled him beneath the waves. This may be the earliest recorded shark attack in history.

Although NYC has less natural historical affinity with barbecue than, say, Dallas or Kansas City, this art is taken very seriously at the establishment. As far as I am concerned, Fette Sau is one of the best addresses for barbecue anywhere on the planet. The restaurant itself is very well appointed. The eastern wall is entirely covered with a fresco from floor to ceiling, illustrating all of the cuts of a cow, pig and lamb, the only animals that Fette Sau barbecues. The rest of the space is beautifully tiled or decorated in a stylish brown with white painted stripes. A monitor showing a sizzling hearth fire provides a homely coziness.

All the tables are set together, and there is no table service, per se. Shenae keeps an eye on everything with utmost efficiency while people stream in and the line of waiting customers gets longer. All the spectacular meat is displayed and you simply order by weight or according to the number of ribs you desire. In addition, you are offered lovely side dishes that constantly vary. One particular hit is the German potato salad and the chili. Try to come here with a group because if you are only two, you will regret not being able to taste all the delicious smoked meat. Fette Sau is truly the king of the NYC barbecue scene.

LUCKY LUNA

167 Nassau Avenue (@Diamond Street) - NY 11222
T (718)383-6038 - www.luckyluna-ny.com
Tues-Sat: Noon - 11:00 p.m., Sun: Noon - 10:00 p.m.

In an almost exclusively Polish street in Greenpoint, three friends managed
to scrape together $28,000 to kick-start their dream. On a corner that previously housed
a pirogi/goulash joint, Lucky Luna became a reality.

Peking duck confit bao buns, Hoisin mayo & chicharrones

The paths of Howard Jang, Ken Ho and Marisa Cadena hardly crossed previously, but once they met again in NYC, they decided to go for it together. Based on their personal experiences, they decided for a fusion concept, incorporating the Taiwanese and Mexican kitchens, seasoned with a Californian touch. Given the scope and significance of Taiwanese and Mexican cuisines, this is a titanic feat. The dishes are inspired by popular street food from both countries. When I look at it from this perspective and especially when I taste the dishes, I believe that Oaxaca and Taipei have more in common than meets the eye. In any case, both kitchens strive for a balance between sweet and spicy, savory meats and crispy vegetables, presented in bite-sized treats.

Lucky Luna is a breath of fresh air. Due to its tight budget, the focus here is totally on the food and not on a bling-bling interior; that is where their efforts really repay dividends. Howard's kitchen is reduced to a sort of "essence" with extraneous elements discarded, and this approach is rare in a city such as NYC. Moreover, he purposely buys his supplies with a priority for local and highly sustainable products. This really gives him the edge when it comes to flavors.

I admire a chef who prefers to buy items externally if he thinks he cannot outdo them himself – and makes no secret of it. For example, he buys his tortillas from the local Tortilleria Nixtamal in Corona, Queens and the buns from Peking Foods in Bushwick, Brooklyn. On the one hand, there is a subtle fusion of two mega-gastronomical cultures, yet sometimes both cultures are presented neatly alongside one another; that does not make for an easy choice. Just give me everything – that is always my initial reaction. If I taste the finesse and depth of the dishes, I can only conclude that this team has ambitions beyond this soberly decorated, low-profile restaurant.

With the Peking duck confit bao, the chef makes no secret of his admiration for the Korean top chef and entrepreneur, David Chang. Chang put this steamed bun on the world map and since then you see this item crop up in every hip joint, typically locked and fully loaded as the carrier of tons of wonderful ingredients. In all fairness, I have to admit that I find this version more captivating than the last steamed bun I sampled at Momofuku. Howard once again delivers an example of perfect balance and delicateness. In the "reverse" carnitas, the meat is first seared and then braised, rather than the other way around, so it arrives unbelievably juicy. The *nec plus ultra* of neighborhood restaurants!

Our kitchen
is bigger than
yours.

...oklynFare.com

CHEF'S TABLE AT BROOKLYN FARE

200 Schermerhorn Street (@ Hoyt Street) - NY 11201
T (718) 243-0050 - www.brooklynfare.com
Open Tues-Wed: 7:00 p.m. and 7:45 p.m., Thurs-Sat:18:00, 18:45, 21:30 and 21:55

Cesar Ramirez is one of the most honorable chefs I know. He has no star-like airs,
nor is he full of himself; he does not do TV, nor does he even prefer to be called a chef;
he thinks of himself rather as a craftsman.

20+ course tasting menu

I think that he secretly fancies himself a shokunin. This autodidact cook is of Mexican descent, born and raised in Chicago. His mentor was David Bouley, and he came to NYC in order to work in Bouley's restaurant.

He married a French woman at the age of 19 and used his many visits to France to learn everything about classic French cuisine and culinary technique. The Chef's Table is the resulting synthesis of Ramirez's culinary formation and of his extensive visits to Japan. According to Ramirez, food should speak for itself, no blah blah. Purity and mastery are his mantras.

Moving from Manhattan to Boerum Hill in Brooklyn was a difficult step, but he entered into a partnership with Moe Issa in order to start a new restaurant together. Issa grew up in this neighborhood and after a successful career as a Pepsi distributor (of all things), dreamed of opening a top delicatessen in this underrated neighborhood full of parking garages. Brooklyn Fare is one of the loveliest gourmet stores I have ever seen, especially because of the decadent selection of products that come from everywhere. Together with Cesar, Issa opened the Chef's Table a few doors down and the rest is gastronomical history.

Certainly owing to the eclectic experience of the chef, the restaurant is unique; only eighteen seats at the bar and nothing else. Makes me think of top sushi bars in Japan – that can't be a coincidence. But the real spectacular act is on the plates. Ramirez is at his best when serving fish and seafood. He flies his sea urchin in directly from Japan, seemingly landing it directly on my plate on a rich brioche and a slice of black truffle. His bouillabaisse gives you a peak into the great French classical repertoire; perfectly fried fugu tails take you back to Japan.

Ramirez has a preference for such luxury products, which have always been associated with haute cuisine. His annual costs for caviar must be enormous. But he reminds me of the sincere and wise priest from the East; whenever I taste his dishes, I am quite convinced he is one of the best food craftsmen on the planet.

BROOKLYN

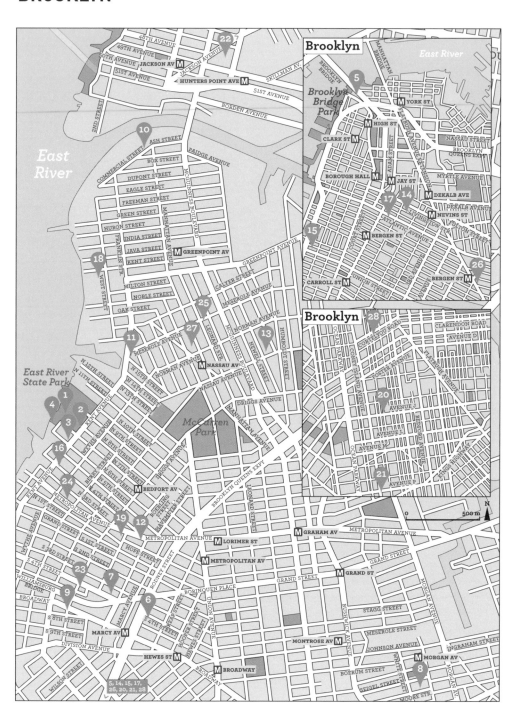

ADDITIONAL EATERIES

15 TAKE ROOT
187 Sackett Street - NY 11231 (Brooklyn)
T +1 347 227 7116
www.take-root.com
▸ **Vegetable driven tasting menu**

16 LANDHAUS AT THE WOODS
48 S 4th Street - NY 11249 (Brooklyn)
T +1 718 710 5020
www.thelandhaus.com
▸ **Poutine with house cut fries**

17 FRENCH LOUIE
320 Atlantic Avenue - NY 11201 (Brooklyn)
T +1 718 935 1200
www.frenchlouienyc.com
▸ **Smoked sardines, dulse butter, rye ficelle**

18 RIVER STYX
21 Greenpoint Avenue - NY 11222 (Brooklyn)
T +1 718 383 8833
www.riverstyxny.com
▸ **Anchovies that have been sitting
   by a fire, chilaquiles**

19 EXTRA FANCY
302 Metropolitan Avenue, NY 11211 (Brooklyn)
T +1 347 422 0939
www.extrafancybklyn.com
▸ **Clam and corn fritters with sriracha ranch dip**

20 DI FARA PIZZA
1424 Avenue J (between 14th and 15th Street)
NY 11230 (Brooklyn)
T +1 718 258 136
www.difara.com
▸ **Calzone**

21 TACIS BEYTI
1955 Coney Island Avenue (between Avenue P &
Kings Highway) - NY 11223 (Brooklyn)
T +1 718 627 5750
www.tacisbeyti.com
▸ **Kiymali pide**

22 BROOKLYN GRANGE
37-18 Northern Boulevard (tbetween 38 and Steinway Street)
NY 11205
T +1 347 670 3660
www.brooklyngrangefarm.com
▸ **Rooftop veggie**

23 PIES AND THIGHS
166 S Fourth Street (Driggs Avenue) - NY 11211
T +1 347 529 6090
www.piesnthighs.com
▸ **Smoked pork hash and eggs**

24 NITEHAWK CINEMA
136 Metropolitan Avenue (between Berry Street and
Whyte Avenue) - NY 11249 (Williamsburg, Brooklyn)
T +1 718 384 3980
www.nitehawkcinema.com
▸ **Crab cakes with avocado mayo**

25 EAT GREENPOINT
124 Meserole Avenue, NY 11222 (Brooklyn)
T +1 718 389 8083
www.eatgreenpoint.com
▸ **Silent meals**

26 MORGANS
267 Flatbush Avenue (corner of St. Marks & Flatbush)
NY 11217 (Brooklyn)
www.morgansbrooklynbarbecue.com
▸ **16h slow smoked brisket**

27 PETER PAN DONUTS AND PASTRY
727 Manhattan Avenue - NY 11222
T +1 718 389 3676
www.peterpan-donuts.com
▸ **Old fashioned cruller donut**

28 CAFE TIBET
1510 Cortelyou Road (Flatbush)
NY 11226
T +1 718 941 2725
▸ **Beef momos**

BRONX

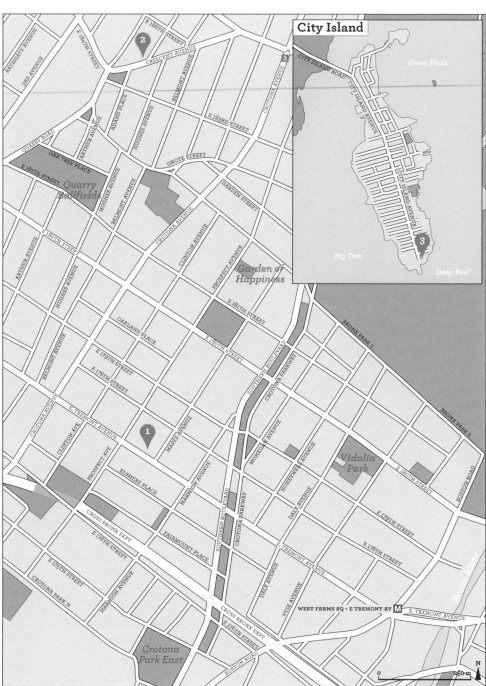

ADDITIONAL EATERIES

1 EL NUEVO BOHIO LECHONERA
791 E Tremont Avenue - NY 10460 (Bronx)
T +1 718 294 3905
www.elnuevobohiorestaurant.com
▸ **Roast pork**

2 ROBERTO
603 Crescent Avenue (Hughes Avenue) - NY 10458
T +1 718 733 9503
www.robertos.roberto089.com
▸ **Pasta e fagioli**

3 JOHNNY'S FAMOUS REEF RESTAURANT
2 City Island Avenue (between Rochelle and the ocean)
NY 10464
T +1 718 885 2086
www.johnnysreefrestaurant.com
▸ **Fried seafood and fried fish**

UPTOWN WEST

ADDITIONAL EATERIES

ASIATE (MANDARIN ORIENTAL HOTEL)
80 Columbus Circle (60th Street, 35th floor) - NY 10023
T +1 212 805 8881
www.mandarinoriental.com/newyork/fine-dining/asiate
▸ **Baby carrots with orange blossom**

PER SE
Time Warner Centre - 10 Columbus Circle
(4th floor, 60th Street) - NY (Broadway)
T +1 212 823 9335
www.perseny.com
▸ **9 course tasting menu**

JEAN-GEORGES
Trump International Hotel
1 Central Park West (between 60th and 61st Streets) - NY 10023
T +1 212 299 3900
www.jean-georges.com
▸ **Jean Georges Menu**

THE EAST POLE

133 E. 65th St. (between Lexington and Park Ave.) - NY 10065
T (212) 249-2222 - www.theeastpolenyc.com
Mon-Fri: 11:30 a.m. - 3:00 p.m., Sat: 10:30 a.m. - noon, Sun: 10:30-23:00

The streets east of Park Avenue on the Upper East Side are a bit odd in terms of restaurants.
Here you can find any type of luxury item that you can possibly imagine, but in the realm
of eateries, the choices are rather limited.

Fish pie

The neighborhood that was known in the mid- 1960s to be the epicenter of *the* singles scene of the city, with T.G.I. Friday's as its locus, was then located on 1st Avenue and 63rd Street. It was thanks to the invention of the "pill" that everyone from all over the city came to this neighborhood to get lucky.

Something seems to be happening again in the East 60s, as if the neighborhood is slowly coming out of its long hibernation and beginning to wake up. The youthful shot that this neighborhood needed seems to have initially come from Brinkley's Station (at 153 E. 60th St.), a partnership between The Fat Radish and the Martignetti brothers, who also operate a gastropub in Soho known as Brinkley's.

But, a further nice surprise was the opening of The East Pole, an uptown restaurant with a downtown feel, housed in a historical brownstone on a quiet block on 65th Street. The bar, which provides mainly standing places, is designed according to a timeless, nautical theme. As a whole, the restaurant is distinguished by simple aesthetics, focusing on the highest quality ingredients.

A chef who can move you with a plate of fresh vegetables, raw and cooked, has caught my full attention, even though I could hardly be thought of as a vegetarian. The man is Nicholas Wilber, a brilliant chef who works unperturbed in his kitchen, never swayed by passing fads. In the morning, he is one of the first at the Union Square Farmers Market, where he knows everyone and has gained their respect as an uncompromising chef who only goes for the best. His macro plate of vegetables – cooked, raw and marinated – changing with the season – is phenomenal. He also has the best connections with farmers, farmsteads and fishermen.

If Nicholas says local, he means local! Unlike some very trendy chefs whose operating radius can be 500 miles, Nicholas buys everything within a 50-mile radius. He believes in building a genuine relationship with his suppliers and partners.

My favorite dish, besides the Scotch egg, is the fish pie, which clearly brings out Nicholas' classic culinary formation. Prepared with puff pastry, this fish pie is a brilliant example of balance in which the fennel (a piquant and assertive element) is kept in check. Magnificent. The East Pole's culinary compass is definitely well-aligned.

ROTISSERIE GEORGETTE

14 E. 60th St. (between Madison Avenue and 5th Avenue) - NY 10022
T (212) 390-8060 - www.rotisserieg.com
Mon-Fri: Noon - 2:30 p.m., Sat: Noon - 3:00 p.m., Tues-Sat: 6.00 p.m. - 11:00 p.m.

Georgette Farkas placed all her culinary trust in top chef, Chad Brauze,
when she started this uptown rotisserie.

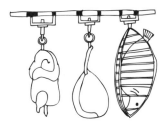

Poule de luxe

Georgette started in the world of restaurants when she was fifteen. After completing hotel school in Switzerland, she went to Monte Carlo to work with Alain Ducasse and later with Daniel Boulud. Seventeen years later, she was ready for her own restaurant.

The idea was very simple, yet not so easy to implement. The key to this restaurant is Chad's partly open kitchen where the wonderfully roasted delights are professionally prepared.

Whole suckling pig, whole lamb or perhaps a leg of lamb, rabbit, a skillfully carved duck or of course the phenomenal roasted chicken, are what you would typically find here. Like many chefs, Chad prefers to roast whole animals or birds, yet he has such complete control of his technique that he seems to add something extra to it; each piece looks tastier than the next. This place serves real food without all sorts of fussy trimmings; it is prepared with real passion for artisanship.

I am glad to see a chef who wants to please his guests with fantastic flavors and not to bluff them with flashy, hi-tech cooking techniques or by offering a taste of things they have never had before. I am actually far more moved by a perfectly grilled leg of chicken than by a tiny piece of chicken on a designer plate, decoratively surrounded by fifteen different mini garnishes. Back to basics has never been so real.

One of the showpieces, the *poule de luxe*, is a full-blooded, free-range pedigreed chicken, with a wonderful filling based on mushrooms, its skin marvelously crispy, the meat just perfectly served with exquisite chicken gravy, wild mushrooms and baked foie gras. This is naturally a decadently delicious dish, served for two, but to be able to eat it, you might even invite your worst enemy.

What I have heard about this restaurant is that it has a refreshing lack of creativity. I am not a great fan of one-liners, but this is a very accurate description of Rotisserie Georgette.

UPTOWN EAST

Central Park
Jacqueline Kennedy Onassis Reservoir
Guggenheim Museum
East River
Jefferson Park
MoMA
96 ST
86 ST
77 ST
72 ST
68 ST - HUNTER COLLEGE
LEXINGTON AV- 63 ST
LEXINGTON AV- 59 ST
5 AV - 59 ST
59 ST
57 ST - 7 AV
5 AV- 53 ST
LEXINGTON AVENUE - 53 ST
51 ST
ROOSEVELT ISLAND
ED KOCH QUEENSBORO BRIDGE
500 m
N

ADDITIONAL EATERIES

FLOCK DINNER
1504 Lexington Avenue - NY 10029
www.flockdinner.com
▸ **Atypical Eating Event with Corey Cova**

SUSHI SEKI
1143 First Avenue (between 62 and 63d Street) - NY 10065
T +1 212 371 0238
www.sushisekinyc.com
▸ **Fried oyster maki**

SHUN LEE PALACE
155 E 55th Street (between Lexington and 3rd Avenue) · NY 10022
T +1 212 371 8844
www.shunleepalace.net
▸ **Peking Duck**

THE JEFFREY
311 E 60th Street (between 1st and 2d Avenue – Roosevelt island
tram station) · NY 10022
T +1 212 355 2337
www.thejeffreynyc.com
▸ **Red beet deviled eggs with House made**
  IPA mustard, chive and dill sriracha

RAO
455 E 114th Street (Pleasant Avenue) · NY
T +1 212 722 6709
www.raos.com
▸ **Mozzarella in carozza**

NOMAD @THE NOMAD HOTEL

1170 Broadway and 28th St. - NY 10001
T (212) 796-1500 - www.thenomadhotel.com/#!/dining
Open Mon-Sun: Noon - 2:00 p.m., Mon - Thurs: 5:30 p.m. -10:30 p.m., Fri-Sat: 5:30 p.m. -11:00 p.m., Sun: 5:30 p.m. -10:00 p.m.

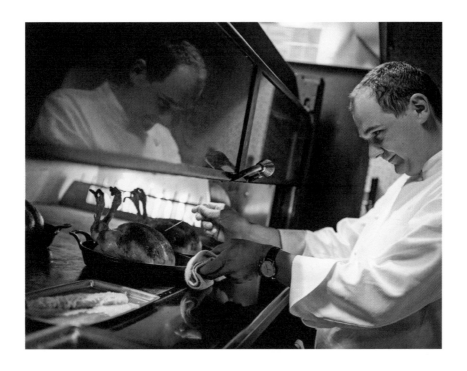

Madison Square Park has always been a public park, as far back
as 1686. NoMad (**No**rth of **Mad**ison Square Park) is a neighborhood
roughly situated between Chelsea, Murray Hill (where numerous
Indian restaurants flourish, creating the recent coinage, "Curry Hill"),
Rose Hill and the Flatiron District.

Chicken

whole-roasted chicken for two, foie gras, black truffle brioche,
white asparagus, soft-poached egg

One of the most iconic buildings in the world is no doubt the Flatiron Building, or the Fuller Building, as it was previously known. This unique building, designed in the Beaux-Arts style in the shape of an iron, has stood there splendidly since 1902 and is one of *the* symbols of NYC.

In this neighborhood where Fifth Avenue and Broadway cross, concealed behind a fine-looking Beaux-Arts façade, is the very beautiful NoMad Hotel, recently renovated to its old grandeur by the French designer, Jacques Garcia. It has a real New York feeling, yet at the same time makes playful reference to the European Grand Hotels. Personally, I find it to be of quite the same caliber as the finest Parisian architecture.

However, the real treasure is the fabulous NoMad restaurant, the prodigious offspring of two super-creative people, Daniel Humm and Will Guidara. The identity of the restaurant is built around key words that were used to define the Rolling Stones (loose, alive, genuine, deliberate); these words are inscribed on the kitchen wall not far from a gigantic photo of Mick Jagger on stage.

In the same neighborhood, the duo also operates Eleven Madison Park, a Michelin 3-star treasure, and for a while the gold standard for restaurants in NYC. But rather than rest on their laurels and launch a simple brasserie in this lovely hotel, they opted for a more adventurous approach: They have taken dishes from the Eleven Madison Park kitchen and transformed them into more magnanimous and openly stylish cuisine. While the dishes at Eleven Madison are meticulously prepared, the culinary equivalent of an old Masters painting rendered with a fine paintbrush, the dishes in NoMad are brushed rapidly with a free hand...

Don't be misled; the food here is incredible and one of the best chicken dishes in NYC can be found in this establishment. You order it for two with someone you care deeply about. This majestic dish is stuffed with a pâte made with the most decadent food groups: brioche dough, truffles and foie gras, and presented whole with a bouquet of herbs, a culinary aphrodisiac of the first order. It looks perfect and tastes even better. Keeping the brioche dough under the skin makes the latter wonderfully crispy and the meat unbelievably juicy. It is prepared as two courses by chef Abram Bissell, who serves this masterpiece as unpretentiously as possible, with only a little mashed potato and sometimes some white asparagus. Followed by a fricassee of morel mushrooms and refreshing desserts, this is a complete meal appreciated by true hedonists. It looks like a dish from yesteryear when great chefs used to really value chicken, yet at the same time, it tastes very contemporary.

Rachel Kerswell, the young and talented sommelier from Quebec, has put together an impressive wine list, which I noticed contains a top selection of New York State wines, not routinely found even on Empire State wine lists. A fabulous culinary spot that can easily become a regular habit.

EISENBERG'S

174 5th Ave. (between 23rd and 22nd St.) - NY 10010
T (212) 675-5096 - www.eisenbergsnyc.com
Open Mon-Fri: 6:30 a.m. - 8:00 p.m., Sat: 9:00 a.m. - 6:00 p.m., Sun: 9:00 a.m. - 5:00 p.m.

Fifth Avenue is one of the most imaginative and inspiring of New York City's arteries.
At the point where it crosses Broadway, in the shadow of the monumental Flatiron building,
you will find an authentic diner/sandwich shop that looks like it has always been there.

Matzo ball soup

de matzahballen worden ingedeeld in floaters en sinkers

On the subject of arterial health, "raising NYC's LDL cholesterol since 1929" has been somewhat of a watchword for this establishment. Amidst all the pomp and splendor of 5th Avenue and its adjacent neighborhoods, this authentic jewel has held its own since 1929. That is in no small part due to the many fans and locals who come here regularly to enjoy the many specialties - tuna melt, Reuben and pastrami sandwiches, and of course, matzo ball soup. Aside from the traditional religious significance for Ashkenazi Jews of eating the unleavened bread of their besieged ancestors in Egypt, and in this case eating hearty chicken broth with two matzo balls floating in it, matzo balls have grown into a tasty and widespread comfort food, especially in traditional diners such as Eisenberg's.

According to the dietary laws in the Torah, proper matzo meal can be made of spelt, rye, oatmeal, wheat or barley flour, and mixed with herbs, parsley, a few egg yokes and lightened (or enlightened) with whipped egg whites, one can be served (if the chef is gifted) a matzo ball of sublime texture and appropriate buoyancy. (Matzo balls are divided into the ontological categories of floaters and sinkers.)

This establishment also zealously guards over the genius invention of Louis Auster, namely, the New York Egg Cream; here it is rigorously and meticulously prepared. Auster was a candy-store owner from Brooklyn and he created a kind of forerunner to the milkshake. The etymology has perhaps been lost in translation; the term may originate from the word, 'egg', but more likely from the Yiddish word, *'echt'* (meaning 'real'). What is certain is that the drink became enormously popular and was perfected by Nathan Herman and Jack Witt, both hailing from Crown Heights, also in Brooklyn. Their traditional egg cream was a mixture of chocolate syrup (Fox's U-Bet can still be found commercially), milk and seltzer; the egg is optional, but it does give an extra dimension to the entire mix. Eisenberg's is one of the last places where you can order this fountain drink, since the recipe can never be bottled.

Plenty of tradition and cultural heritage await you at this cozy diner where you are guaranteed to strike up a conversation with one of the many locals who feast there on Reuben or pastrami sandwiches. You won't find many super-cool dudes with beards and tattooed forearms or buns in their hair, but authenticity reigns here. Aida, Eisenberg's very charming hostess, will efficiently help you find your way around this unique world of tastes.

EATALY NYC

200 5th Ave. (between 23rd and 24th St.) - NY 10010
T (212) 229-2560 - www.eataly.com/nyc

Open daily: 10:00 a.m.-11:00 p.m. (coffee bar from 8:00 p.m.)

Stepping into Eataly NYC has always been somewhat overwhelming for me. Very rarely do I find
so many uncompromised quality products under one roof. In this gigantic, virtually
hallucinogenic mega-store, they have indeed managed to offer the quality and ingredients
that can only be found in small-scale artisanal shops in Italy.

Parmigiano reggiano

How they achieved this is actually very simple: they turned their passion and hobby into a profession and even on this scale, they are just as passionate about using top ingredients. This is the plain secret behind the success of Eataly.

There are twenty-seven Eataly shops in Italy, thirteen in Japan, one in Turkey, one in Chicago, one in Dubai, but *the* Eataly shop is on 5th Avenue in New York City. Eataly is certainly the best ambassador that Italy could have ever have dreamed of, as it presents the very best The Boot has to offer. Buffalo milk magically transformed into a ball of super mozzarella, breads made from the very best flour and baked in the best ovens, *the* freshest of fish, freshly prepared pasta, unbelievably fine meat products, cheeses from top producers. The very finest Italian everything is curated at this definitive, artisanal quality market.

Getting hungry from just looking at all these delicious products? (Anyone who doesn't get hungry here should see a doctor urgently.) No problem. One of the many restaurants under this roof will offer an instant solution: a masterly pizza, a perfect *panino*. The various little restaurants will make your taste buds swear they were in Italy. Taste the fish specialties, pastas and amazing rotisserie. There is even a Nutella bar...

The key word in Eataly NY is harmony, and it was for this reason that I opted for their truly remarkable *parmigiano reggiano* cheese. Why? Because Parmesan cheese often acts as the liaison between Italian dishes, traditional or modern. *Parmigiano Reggiano* comes from the Parma region and has been produced there since 1200, always in the same fashion. You need about sixteen liters of milk to produce one kilo of cheese, therefore about six hundred liters are needed for one large ball weighing in around 80 pounds. Every cow – and there are around 300,000 in the region – makes ten to eleven cheeses per year. The milk with the most characteristic taste comes from the *vacca rossa*. In Eataly NY you will find only the very best quality, known as *prima stagionatura*. The diversity found at Eataly is incredible, and for me, reflects the enormous diversity of the Italian kitchen.

ELEVEN MADISON PARK

11 Madison Avenue - NY 10010
T (212) 889-0905 - info@elevenmadisonpark.com
Open Mon-Sun: 5:30 p.m.-10:00 p.m., Thurs-Sat (lunch): 12:00 p.m.- 1:00 p.m. - Reservations: Mon-Sat: 9:00 a.m.- 6:00 p.

Magnificently handsome buildings with distinctive Art Deco influences line the small but extraordinarily beautiful Madison Park. The showpiece is naturally the Fuller Building or the Flatiron Building as it is currently called.

Tasting menu

Daniel Humm's work continues to surprise both friends and foes

One of these beautiful façades, specifically the former Metropolitan Life Building (now the Credit Suisse building), conceals perhaps the most heralded restaurant in NYC: Eleven Madison Park. In 2006, owner Danny Meyer took the brilliant step of bringing chef Daniel Humm on board this ambitious venture. They quickly realized that together they had created a marvelous synergy and would soon be Kings of the City. For their opening in 1998, a wine list was developed with sufficient depth, and of course the setting – the beautiful room – had all the qualities needed to create a memorable restaurant. It was only the food that needed a bit of a boost.

At the age of 25, Daniel Humm of Switzerland had already earned one Michelin star at the Gasthaus Zum Gupf in the Alps. He had made a great impression on Danny Meyer, who was then also the owner of Gramercy Tavern and Union Square Café when they met at Campton Place in San Francisco. The dream team hired Will Guidara as general manager and John Ragan as the wine director. After Daniel Humm and Will Guidara bought Eleven Madison Park from Danny Meyer in 2011, they made the final format switch that made the place what it is today. The restaurant no longer features an à la carte concept, but rather a fantastically daring and surprising tasting menu that tests the imaginative boundaries of your taste buds.

Daniel Humm's work continues to surprise both friends and foes. His carrot tartare is truly amazing and continues to entertain diners: two carrots are ground in a meat grinder attached to your table, then seasoned to taste with various condiments you have selected, accompanied with a quail egg yolk. His creations are personal and with few trimmings; like a stealth bomber, you are blown away by the flavor, balance and depth of the preparations. A truly unique experience. And then there is the magical trick with playing cards at dessert time...

IVAN RAMEN

EL COLMADO >

WINE >

Ivan Ramen
slurp shop

The Art of the Slurp

IVAN RAMEN SLURP SHOP

600 11th Ave. (between 44th and 45th St.) - NY 10036
T (212) 582-7942 - www.ivanramen.com/en/ivan-ramen-slurp-shop
Open daily: 11:30 a.m. - 10:00 p.m.

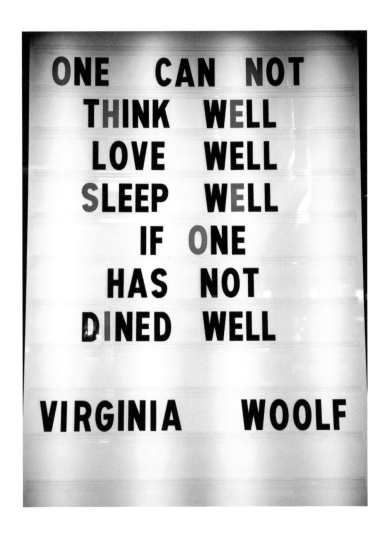

Ivan Ramen is a Japanese ramen noodle bar in the Setagaya quarter in Tokyo; its owner
and the driving force behind the bar is chef Ivan Orkin, originally from Syosset, NY.

Tokyo shio ramen soup

Slurp till you drop!

Ivan lived for many years in Japan and was totally smitten by the complexity of its culinary world. He was especially enchanted by his observation of the refining of the delicate broth used as the basis for Japan's "simple" but wonderful ramen soup. Although he is considered a *gaijin* (foreigner in Japanese), Ivan Orkin dared to open a ramen bar squarely in the lion's den. Initially, the Japanese were very skeptical, but quite rapidly word got around that this *gaijin* really knew his noodles (and broth). A winning rich bouillon and handmade noodles were seemingly all you needed to make great ramen, but it is not as simple as it may seem. This is evidenced by the page-long ramen recipe in his lovely new book, *Love, Obsession and Recipes.*

Fantastic ramen soup is on a strong revival path everywhere, but primarily in NYC where good ramen bars are springing up one after the other. Ivan now has two locations in NYC where people can find his version of the Tokyo shio ramen. The more striking of the two is in Hell's Kitchen, more specifically in the new and spectacular Gotham West Market, which you might sooner call industrial. But don't be fooled by the location; this is by no means an industrial product.

The Tokyo shio ramen is skillfully prepared, based in a hearty rich-layered dashi/chicken broth made with Japanese sea salt, handmade rye noodles and very delicate chashu pork of exceptional depth and complexity. The noodles are cooked to perfection and taste like... I want more. The delicate pork meat melts in your mouth and the creamy yolk provides the finishing touch. A sensation.

Recently, a second location has opened in the Lower East Side at 25 Clinton Street. Slurping is certainly permitted here; in fact, it is very much encouraged.

CHELSEA MARKET

75 9th Ave. (between 15th and 16th St.) - NY 10011
T (212) 652-2110 - www.chelseamarket.com
Open Mon-Sat: 7:00 a.m. - 9:00 p.m., Sun: 8:00 a.m. - 8:00 p.m.

A walk through the old Oreo building, which houses the Chelsea Market,
is one of the quickest ways to feel like a New Yorker.

Local vendors

This building is related to the eponymous cookies; since 1890, all sorts of cookies have been baked in this small factory. From 1990 the building was used for other purposes and offices were set up in the top floors, but what is really interesting is the eclectic mix of food shops, small restaurants and bakeries. The atmosphere here is very homey and everyone walks around enjoying themselves, leisurely chatting with one another. There is lots of eating and it is certainly good eating. The location, by the way, has a historical connection to the production and distribution of food that dates back to the Algonquin Indians and their trade in wild animals and crops. The High Line served the local meat traders and butchers (after all, we are in the middle of the Meatpacking District) before it ultimately became a cookie building. Currently, there are around 35 shops operating in the Chelsea Market and around six million people find their way to this place each year.

The diversity of the offerings is immense and I find it to be a fantastic place for breakfast, brunch or lunch. Stroll along the shops and let yourself be enticed by a homemade donut, a perfectly poached lobster, homemade cold cuts, ice cream, or an espresso. Truly a unique place for just letting go for a while...

MORIMOTO

88 10th Ave. (between 15th and 16th St.) - NY 10011
T (212) 989-8883 - www.morimotonyc.com
Open Mon-Fri: Noon - 2:30 p.m., Mon -Wed: 5:30 p.m.-11:00 p.m., Thurs-Sat: 5:30 p.m. -midnight and Sun: 5:30 p.m.-10:00 p.m.

Iron Chef Masaharu Morimoto is a traditionally trained Japanese chef from Hiroshima,
where he formerly owned his own restaurant but sold it in 1985 because he wanted
to introduce fusion style cuisine.

*only the fattiest part
of the tuna is used*

Toro tartare with caviar

After a short stint as a chef at Nobu, it was time for him to open his own restaurants, first in Philadelphia and later here in Chelsea.

The design of this monumental restaurant is stunning, extremely beautiful with lots of room and light, but the spectacular achievement of this Japanese oasis is clearly its top-quality kitchen. At the head of the team is the young and very talented chef, Erik Battes, who certainly infuses the philosophy of the house into all the dishes that are served. I am constantly amazed at how the staff manages to create such a plethora of complex Japanese preparations for such a large number of enthusiastic diners. Here the plates are dressed up with frightful precision.

The kitchen has further developed its own style – thanks to the perceptive diligence of Erik Battes. Although the dishes are still very much Japanese, the kitchen incorporates subtle touches

from other gastronomical vernaculars. Japanese dishes are reviewed and restyled, but what is ultimately served comes straight from the mind and heart of a chef who clearly knows what he wants.

One of the things you want to do before you shuffle off this mortal coil is to experience Chef Battes' sublime o-toro tartare, which contains only the fattiest part of the tuna. Nowadays, o-toro, which literally means melting, is considered a superb delicacy, yet even in Japan this has become the case only recently. Before WWII, when fat was considered taboo in Japan, you could go to the Tsukiji fish market and pick up pieces for feeding your cat. Erik Battes prepares his o-toro tartare in an extremely pure traditional fashion, but adds to the lovely plate a variety of seasonings and condiments so that diners can experiment and decide what goes best with the subtle meat of a top o-toro.

THE HALAL GUYS

10-02 34th Avenue - Astoria, NY 11106 - T (347) 527-1505
53rd St. and 6th Ave.: 'Original Location' 7:00 a.m.- 4:00 p.m. (Fri-Sat: until 5:00 p.m.)
53rd St. and 6th Ave.: 10:00 a.m. - 4:00 p.m. (Fri-Sat: until 5:00 p.m.)
53rd St. and 7th Ave.: 10:00 a.m. - 5:00 p.m.
307 E 14th St.: 10:00 a.m. - 4:00 a.m., Fri-Sat: until 5:30 a.m.

Whenever you see a long line in Manhattan,
it is usually for a taxi or a street food cart with superb food.

Gyros/chicken on rice

a legendary food cart!

These guys even have bouncers to make sure that there are no fights, as was the case in October 2006 when a person was stabbed to death because another person accused him of jumping the line.

Since establishing their business spots in 1990, the Halal Guys (or Chicken & Rice or 53rd & 6th, as they are known by the locals) have been creating long lines at their various locations in the Theater District of Manhattan. Mohammed Abouelenein, an Egyptian, originally began with a hot dog stand, but got so little satisfaction from his work that barely two years later he switched to a formula that is still successful today: gyros and/or chicken with rice. Their secret ingredient is the white sauce, which looks somewhere between mayonnaise and yoghurt, and adds a special flavor to the slightly spicy gyros.

Gyros is traditionally Greek and consists of grilled beef or lamb meat, cut into strips and seasoned. It looks like shoarma or taco al pastor (taco cut from the spit). All three derive from the Turkish Döner Kebab, which originated from Bursa sometime during the 19th century.

The popularity of this food cart knows no limits. I heard a very well-known NYC chef say that one Christmas evening he stood for two and a half hours in line in the cold. At New York University, a student club was established recently, whose members are wild about this legendary food cart.

BUDDAKAN

75 9th Ave. (@16th St.) - NY 10011
T (212) 989-6699 - www.buddakannyc.com

Open Mon: 5:30 p.m. - 11:00 p.m., Tues-Wed: 5:30 p.m. - midnight, Thurs-Fri: 5:30 -1:00 a.m., Sat: 5:00 p.m. - 1:00 a.m., Sun: 5:00 p.m. - 11:00 p.m.

When I first came here, I didn't get the impression that I was stepping into a restaurant, but rather had been invited to the semi-evacuated property of one or another eccentric Cantonese billionaire, working for SPECTRE.

Crispy soft shell crab, jicama, watermelon, nuoc mam

I went down the stairs, which led through the central dining area, stately decorated with Chinoiserie wallpaper, and descended into the catacombs, which seem as though they lead to the central safe where it all takes place.

The fact that Buddakan is no ordinary place is noticeable from the moment you enter and find yourself squeezing past NYC's most beautiful people, their faces dimly illuminated by their smartphones, as they call their dates, triangulating on their likely ETAs. My date, the iconic winemaker Egon Müller from the Saar and by coincidence in the city for the NY Wine Experience, had apparently already arrived. The French designer Christian Liaigre, whose design projects include The Market for Jean-Georges Vongerichten in Paris, drew up the plans for a type of Chinese Estate on steroids.

The theme of this mega-XL nightclub/restaurant is the modern Asian kitchen. Most of the time this boils down to disastrous execution, but chef Michael Schulson will make us reconsider. After all, Buddakan is located close to Chinatown, so the inevitable comparison will be made. My experience has taught me that if this is the food you get in a typical Chinatown eatery, you should count yourself lucky.

The choice of dim sum is good and for the most part tastes very authentic. My favorite is a wonderful illustration from the innovative Asian fusion kitchen. Crispy soft shell crabs with a refreshing and crispy salad made from jicama and watermelon in which the sweetness is balanced by the just right quantity of Thai fish sauce. By the way, jicama or yamboon is becoming very popular. This tuber, shaped like a top, is white on the inside, sweet-tasting and deliciously crunchy. The menu changes frequently, but the staff lets you get acquainted with the classical dishes.

TORO

85 10th Avenue - NY 10011
T (212) 691-2360 - www.toro-nyc.com
Mon-Wed: 5:30 p.m. - 11:00 p.m., Thurs-Sun: 5:30 p.m. - midnight

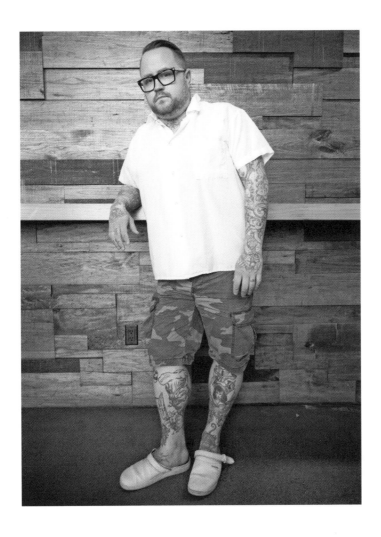

The very small but quiet 14th St. Park is located in the shadow of another fantastic park,
The High Line, and appears to be the virtual front yard of Toro.

Morcilla de cordero con habas

for such tapas most Barcelona tapas bars would have to rise very early

In earlier times, cookies were baked here, as was the neighboring Chelsea Market. Because of the open space that surrounds the restaurant, this place takes on a very dynamic aspect, a sort of Chelsea incarnation of a busy tapas bar in Barcelona. The retention of the elements that accentuate its industrial history and the large windows offering a wonderful cityscape, give the restaurant an extra vivid sense of liveliness. The diversity of the interior arrangement gives you a choice of intimate dining for two or a tapas feast with friends, your table overflowing with wine porrons.

As the name intimates, the kitchen focuses on both modern and traditional Spanish tapas. Many local Spanish flavors and techniques are smoothly combined here with local, fresh produce. Whenever I taste their tapas, I start to wonder if Chef Jamie Bissonnette has some Spanish blood in his veins; for such tapas, most Barcelona tapas bars would have to rise really early. A monumental example in my opinion is his bocadillo de erizos or sea urchin sandwich. It's a pity it's not always available owing to the irregular supply of this delicious ingredient. If you see it on recommended dishes, don't even think twice.

One of my favorite places in Barcelona is an eighty year old family charcuterie shop called La Pineda in Carrer del Pi. It is the fantasy of any meat lover and looks as though its owners and patrons live in their own unique time zone. It is a tiny place with an interior consisting of only a few rickety chairs and tables, and lots of Iberian top cured hams as well as other cultural relics. Although located in Barrio Gòtico, you rarely see any tourists here. I always leave the place with a glorious feeling and an overloaded shopping bag. For me, these are the real souvenirs from Barcelona. But it is the morcilla (blood sausage) made from lamb blood that really leaves the most deeply imprinted memory of this unique place.

I always get great pleasure from knowing that Jamie Bissonnette makes his morcillas just like the ones I remember from Spain. The morcilla is briefly cooked and combined with a steaming pot of fava beans. This combination becomes even more magnificent by the addition of fresh sheep milk's ricotta. Barcelona and NYC have therefore more in common than just the statue of Christopher Columbus: a fantastic tapas bar!

BODEGA NEGRA

W 16th St. (between 8th and 9th Ave.) - NY 10011
T (212) 229-2336 - www.bodeganegranyc.com
Sun-Wed: 5:30 p.m. - midnight, Thurs-Sat: 5:30 p.m. - 1:00 a.m.

Mexican cuisine is probably the most underrated cuisine in the world,
although it did receive the flashy UNESCO world heritage protectorate.

Yellowtail ceviche, coconut ginger, mango, habanero salsa

I'm always distraught by the fact that we tend to associate this richly diverse cuisine with an inferior and inedible cuisine, replete with bad corn and a mush that has come to pass for refried beans.

Mexican cuisine is a successful marriage between the native Mesoamerican cuisine and certain Spanish influences, gracias to the Spanish conquest of the Aztecs. As befitting true imperialists, the Spanish tried to completely impose their own culinary world on their subjects, but that did not succeed so well; ultimately other ingredients and cooking techniques spontaneously mixed in, evolving into a far greater and more complex whole. This is how many local variants, such as Oaxaca, Veracruz and Yucatan cuisine, began to emerge.

Serge Becker, together with Will Ricker and Ed Spencer Churchill, decided that the Dream Downtown hotel would be the best NYC venue for their Bodega Negra concept. While their London version looks more like a sex shop/peep show (oh, those repressed Anglo-Saxons), the choice here was for a

Mexican fever dream, complete with mariachi guitars, stacked-up wooden tequila barrels, a disco ball made of coins, lots of copper and mirrors. The south-of-the-border interior is whimsical and frivolous and the perfect decor for the most trendy Mexican restaurant in NY.

Ex-Morimoto, Michael Armstrong is the chef and he guarantees a very impressive menu, mainly based on inspiration from his favorite Yucatan cuisine. Armstrong's mentor is Diana Kennedy, the renowned specialist in regional Mexican cuisine. Many Mexican classics are a bit restyled, but without compromising their vibrant culinary power. The quesadillas with habanero and roasted tomato come quite close to a good pizza experience, while the taco with soft-shell crab, as well as the one made with Peking duck, are brilliant inventions. Bodega Negra is a real cultural ambassador of Mexican cuisine. Furthermore, it is a favorite place to stop before advancing further into the night to the fantastic Electric Room, just a few doors down.

MIDTOWN WEST

ADDITIONAL EATERIES

 OOTOYA CHELSEA
8 W 18th Street (between 5th Avenue and 6th Avenue)
NY 10011
T +1 212 255 0018
www.ootoya.us
▸ Rosu katsu teishoku

ANEJO TEQUILERIA
668 10th Avenue (47th Street) · NY
T +1 212 920 4770
www.anejonyc.com
▸ Tlayuda

CITY SANDWICH
649 Ninth Avenue · NY 10036
T +1 646 684 3943
www.citysandwichnyc.com/
▸ Portuguese sandwiches

MAREA
240 Central Park South (between Broadway and 7th Avenue)
NY 10019
T +1 212 582 5100
www.marea-nyc.com
▸ Strozzapreti, jumbo crab, sea urchin, basil

 ROBERTS AT THE PENTHOUSE CLUB
603 W 45th Street (between 11th and 12th)
T +1 212 245 0002
www.penthouseclubny.com/steakhouse.nxg
▸ Porterhouse and onion rings

 DAISY MAY'S BBQ USA
623 11th Avenue (46th Street) · NY 10017
T +1 212 977 1500
www.daisymaysbbq.com
▸ Pork butt

 GRAMERCY TAVERN
42 East 20th Street (between Broadway an
Park Avenue south) NY 10003
T +1 212 477 0777
www.gramercytavern.com
▸ Corn custard, sungold tomatoes
and shishito peppers

 PAM REAL THAI
404 West 49th Street · NY 10019
T +1 212 333 7500
www.pamrealthaifood.com
▸ Oxtail soup

SUSHI YASUDA

204 E 43rd St. (between 2nd and 3rd Avenue) - NY 10017
T (212) 972-1001 - www.sushiyasuda.com
Open Mon-Fri: Noon - 2:15 p.m. and 6:00 p.m. - 10:15 p.m., Sat: 6:00 p.m. - 10:15 p.m.

"My life will never be the same," said a good friend of mine after he had his first uni sushi at Yasuda. You can't say I hadn't warned him. He had made his way through countless Japanese eateries, but never outside of Europe, and clearly, he was now playing (or at least spectating) in a different league.

Uni sushi —• sea urchin

Naomichi Yasuda established Sushi Yasuda in 2000 together with Shige Akimoto and Scott Rosenberg and they struck gold from day one. They had the whole proper sushi Gestalt: minimalist, whitewood decor, Japanese hierarchical standards of fanatical quality and precision in the kitchen, fish and seafood flown in from all corners of the globe, a vibrant essential sake list and an immensely driven and talented chef – Yasuda himself.

Many people refuse to believe or simply cannot imagine that it takes ten to fifteen years to master the art of making perfect sushi. Sushi has a very long history that has evolved over time, and one is sometimes privileged to taste the results of these incremental advances of civilized gastronomy. In Japan, if you want to be taken seriously as a sous-chef, you have to practice for many years and only the very best ever attain the status of being *shokunin*, a national treasure, granted only to those who achieve a higher order of excellence through artisanal craftsmanship. I have rarely tasted this level of perfection outside of Japan, but Yasuda hits the mark each time.

Eating sushi must be a complete and sensory experience. Everything must be in place. Stepping into Yasuda means taking a break from the frenetic madness of Midtown East – the restaurant is located just a few steps from Grand Central Station. It feels like you are entering a magical bubble, stepping into a Japanese cocoon. As a welcoming gesture, you are given a glass of water filtered through *binchotan* (rare Japanese charcoal made from centennial oak trees) into a carafe. This establishment is always full, yet the staff retains an eerie level of serenity and poise. These sushi chefs are at one with what they do; they act as a medium for their product, the catalyst that transforms rice and fish into a magical tasting experience. They are capable of extreme focus – think of Japanese photography – which it seems only the Japanese can do with this level of precision. A perfect sushi is a synergistic microcosm that tastes far more complex than its separate ingredients. In this place, every sushi is an experience, a mini-tasting menu in one bite. It begins with the feather-light rice resembling a fluffy cloud, and makes you wonder how the chef succeeds in having the rice grains stick together while constantly keeping their temperature lukewarm.

The choice of super fresh and skillfully handled fish is staggering, making your selection a serious problem. Recommendations are *mirugai* (giant clam), *anago*, Spanish mackerel, *sayori*, cherrystone clam, *hotategai himo* (the spines of sea scallops), and of course, *uni*, the famed, highly erotic sea urchin! The *uni* sushi, or *maki* with *uni* is one of the best bites that you will ever experience in Manhattan.

Initially disorienting, but typical of all top sushi bars, is the absence of soy sauce on the table, because every sushi is made by the master with the quantity of soy sauce that he considers necessary and appropriate. Also typical is the artistically folded finger napkins; after all, you eat sushi with your hands, or better, with your fingers.

Mitsuru Tamura, who worked as the sous-chef for eleven years, took over the task of chef in 2011 when Yasuda went back to Japan to open a sushi bar in Tokyo. Sushi Yasuda is probably the best sushi bar outside of Japan.

HAANDI

113 Lexington Ave. (between 27th and 28th St.) - NY 10016
T (212) 685-5200 - www.facebook.com/Haandi-NYC
Open daily 10:00 a.m. - 4:00 a.m.

If you live in Manhattan without a car and feel like having real Indian cuisine, you may think that you have to hike all the way to Jackson Heights in New Jersey or to Floral Park in Queens. However, there is a sort of mini-Little India close by.

Chicken tikka

The small area of Murray Hill, around 28th Street and Lexington Avenue is very affectionately known as Curry Hill, given the presence of many Indian restaurants there. Here you will find everything that India has to offer, from dosa to Pakistani kebabs, and a very rich and tasty South Indian market.

I am totally addicted to chicken prepared in any conceivable way. Just as I find that the Japanese unagi or kabayaki is the best eel dish in the world, I think that by far the best and most intriguing chicken dish is chicken tikka. The scent, the look, and of course the taste cannot be compared to any other prepared chicken that I know. Chicken tandoori is inextricably associated with India, yet this complex taste explosion originated elsewhere, namely in the Persian Mughal Empire that ruled North India between approximately 1526 and 1757. The rulers were direct descendants of Genghis Khan. The influence of this kingdom was immense; approximately 150 million people were already living in the area at that time.

The dominant cuisine was named after the Muslim Mughlai Empire, operating in the Iranian Kashmir and Punjab regions. Tandoori chicken became popular mainly among the Muslim population at the time when the Mughal Empire fell apart.

The dish found its way into the hearts of North Indians and Pakistanis, and straight into my heart, too. A cut chicken thigh is marinated in yoghurt, lime or lemon juice, along with a mixture of fresh herbs and spices, and is magically transformed by its tenure in the tandoori oven into a piece of emotion. The effect of the yoghurt and lime or lemon juice on the chicken makes the meat very tender. A brief baking time in a traditional, very hot tandoori (900 to 1100 degrees F.) is enough to produce a fire-red chicken thigh that will always give you a different perspective on chicken.

Ali, the very friendly owner of Haandi, keeps a firm hand on the business. I first went into the restaurant because I saw many Indian taxi chauffeurs sitting there enjoying their food. For many North Indian chauffeurs, this is an essential part of their day, just like filling their automobiles with gas. What an amazing discovery! Apart from the buffet, you can also order a large variety of specialties à la carte from the kitchen. For the adventurous diners (temperamental if not direct descendants of Genghis Khan), there is the Magaz masala, split goat-head curry in which the cheeks, tongue and especially the brains are eaten from the skull. Haandi's kebabs are perfectly seasoned and have a nice texture, but for its chicken tikka and tandoori I will gladly go the extra mile.

Central Park

E 62ND STREET
E 63RD STREET
5 AV - 59 ST
8
Lexington Av - 63 St
57 ST - 7 AV
57 ST
E 60TH STREET
7 AV
E 62ND STREET
50 ST
W 58TH STREET
Lexington Av - 59 St
W 56TH STREET
59 ST
MoMA
50 ST
E 57TH STREET
49 ST
W 52ND STREET
5 AV - 53 ST
E 56TH STREET
47ST - 50ST
E 55TH STREET
Times
Square
W 48TH STREET
Lexington Avenue - 53 St
W 46TH STREET
51 ST
E 51ST STREET
42 ST - PORT AUTHORITY
E 50TH STREET
42 ST - TIMES SQ
E 46TH STREET
42 ST - TIMES SQ
W 43RD STREET
42 ST - BRYANT PARK
5 AV
Bryant
Park
Grand
Central
Terminal
E 45TH STREET
Chrysler
Building
1
34 ST - PENN STATION
GRAND CENTRAL - 42 ST
E 44TH STREET
E 43RD STREET
GRAND CENTRAL - 42 ST
W 39TH STREET
Penn
Station
4
E 39TH STREET
United Nations
Building
34 ST - HERALD SQ
W 34TH STREET
E 38TH STREET
Empire State
Building
E 40TH STREET
28 ST
33 ST
E 32ND STREET
St. Vartan's
Park
23 ST
9
E 31ST STREET
East
River
Madison
Square
Park
6
5   2
28 ST
E 27TH STREET
E 26TH STREET
23 ST
E 26TH STREET
3
23 ST
10
E 22ND STREET
E 19TH STREET
Gramercy
Park
7
E 21ST STREET
Union
Square
Park
14 ST - UNION SQ

N
0   500 m

ADDITIONAL EATERIES

3 THE GANDER
15 W 18th Street, NY 10011
T +1 212 229 9500
www.thegandernyc.com
▸ Beef brisket tots

4 KAJITSU
125 E 39th Street (between Lex and Park)
T +1 212 228 4873
www.kajitsunyc.com
▸ Shojin inspired omakase

5 DHABA
108 Lexington Avenue (between 27 and 28), NY 10016
T +1 212 679 1284
www.dhabanyc.com
▸ Punjab da murgh

6 TIFFIN WALLAH
127 East 28th Street (between Lexington and Park), NY
T +1 212 685 7301
www.tiffindelivery.us
▸ South Indian specialties

7 UNION SQUARE CAFÉ
21 East 16th Street (between 5th Avenue and
Union Square West), NY 10003
T +1 212 243 4020
www.unionsquarecafe.com
▸ Crispy Soft Shell Crab, spicy Tomato Sauce,
  Zucchini, Basil, Lemon Aiol

8 AUREOLE
34 East 61st Street, NY 10036
T +1 212.319.1660
www.charliepalmer.com/aureole_new-york
▸ Tasting menu

9 PENELOPE
159 Lexington Avenue, NY 10016
T +1 212 481 3800
www.penelopenyc.com
▸ Chicken pot pie

10 MAIALINO
2 Lexington Avenue, NY 10010
T +1 212 777 2410
www.maialinonyc.com
▸ Chocolate croissant bread pudding

SPICE MARKET

403 West 13th St. (corner of 9th Ave.) - NY 10014
T (212) 675-2322 - www.spicemarketnewyork.com
Open Sun-Wed: 11:30 a.m. - midnight, Thurs-Sat: 11:30 a.m. - 1:00 a.m.

I have profound admiration for Jean-Georges Vongerichten for various reasons, but mainly because he is an incredibly versatile chef with an open mind, the kind you rarely meet, certainly among those who were lucky enough to have had a purely classical education.

Spiced chicken samosa and cilantro yoghurt

This native of Alsace grew up close to Strasbourg and perfected his skills working with a few of the great classical, top French chefs such as Paul Haeberlin (Auberge de l'Ill) and Paul Bocuse, one of the greatest of his generation.

Jean-Georges probably developed his fascination with eastern flavors a long time ago, but this obsession, if you will, may have first manifested when he opened his first Vong, establishing a new standard in fusion cooking. The Spice Market was opened in 2003 after three intensive years of searching for spices. I have frequently eaten in his restaurants around the world and in my opinion there are two things in which Vongerichten really excels. On the one hand, he is a master of combining spices, seasoning and ingredients, whether you eat at his three-star Michelin restaurant or at his Spice Market. This is a rather remarkable accomplishment. He also, no less importantly, has shown the talent to find the right people everywhere he operates and to motivate them to perform at the highest levels. In this way, he was able to rope in Wim Van Gorp in Paris for The Market.

The word samosa comes from the Persian sanbosag, the earliest references dating back to the 10th century. The Iranian historian Abolfazl Bayhaqi (995-1075) mentions them in his writings and they spread worldwide via Arab traders in the 13th and 14th centuries.

Throughout history, samosas have been regularly mentioned in writings; songs were composed praising their tastiness. Amir Khusro, a poet in the court of the sultan of Delhi, also describes the ingredients in his poems; he mentions meat, ghee, onions, almonds and spices. The Ain-i-Akbari, an important culinary and cultural heritage document of the Mughal from the 16th century, literally contains the recipe for qutab, which the Hindus call sanbusah. A samosa is a very popular snack/lunch in North India and Pakistan and by now has extended to the entire Arabic-speaking world, Turkey, Goa, Portugal...

In the monumental and sexy Spice Market NY, Anthony Ricco supervises everything. Here the filling is based on chicken and has the ultimate balance of spices. The texture is also exemplary. This samosa with a bit of delicious yoghurt sauce is one of the most delicious things that you can eat in NY; it will eternally have a special place in my heart.

You simply can't go wrong here in your selection, because every dish exemplifies the same subtle balance. The sea bass tempura steamed buns with peanuts and crispy herbs, for example, is also a dish that is exquisitely balanced and will hauntingly spice your dreams.

NAKAZAWA SUSHI

23 Commerce St. (between Bedford St. and 7th Ave. South) - NY 10014
T (212) 924-2212 - www.sushinakazawa.com
Open Mon-Sat: 5:00 p.m. -10:00 p.m.

This is a difficult issue for me: Where can I find the best sushi in NYC?
There are two places that ascend above the rest: Yasuda and Nakazawa.

eating here is a magical moment

Omakase sushi

There is no limit to what television can do! Sometime in August 2012, when Alessandro Borgognone, plopped down on his couch after work in his Italian restaurant and saw a documentary about Jiro Ono (Jiro Dreams of Sushi), the best sushi chef in the world, he was absolutely blown off his rocker by the work ethic and pure craftsmanship of sushi-making. Daisuke Nakazawa was presented several times in this documentary as the most talented and diligent student who had ever worked in the most rigorous restaurant, Sukiyabashi Jiro. That same evening Borgognone contacted Nakazawa – with some help from Google Translate (no less), and in August 2013 Sushi Nakazawa became a fact. Aside from both having clean-shaven heads, Borgognone and Nakazawa don't seem to have much in common, but somehow the two have established a magical bond. Nakazawa is the utmost sophisticated sushi chef, who had to make more than two hundred tamagodashi day after day for his teacher before the latter found them acceptable.

In this quiet tree-lined street in West Village, Nakazawa serves only omakase sushi, a type of tasting menu consisting of 20 sorts of sushi and a temaki. By now, his strict Japanese sushi style has made way for a type of *New York-mae*, a fusion of the best of both worlds.

One hundred minutes of pure heaven is what awaits you if you are one of the lucky people who manage to reserve a table. I had to treat my swollen finger from pressing incessantly on the redial button in order to make a reservation and you would really be crazy not to do it too. Twenty-one courses of sushi from the best waters in the world, freshly flown in, handmade by a genuine, top-master of fish – who additionally has the talent of making a small heap of top-quality rice laid under perfectly cut pieces of fish – feel like a fluffy cloud. Nakazawe is always pleased to show you on his tablet a picture of any fish or seafood that you aren't familiar with. Eating here is a magical moment, as if you have been released from a heavy burden.

DOMINIQUE ANSEL BAKERY

189 Spring St. (between Sullivan and Thompson St.) - NY 10012
T (212) 219-2773 - www.dominiqueansel.com
Mon-Sat: 8:00 a.m. - 7:00 p.m., Sun: 9:00 a.m. - 7:00 p.m.

Not many bakeries can add revolutionary new items to an already extensive repertoire. To do that and to create perhaps the most febrile buzz the culinary world has experienced in a very long time, in an arena as critical and demanding as NYC, surely suggests that we are talking about an incredibly gifted professional: top French baker, Dominique Ansel.

Cronut

What is clear is that traveling a lot with an open mind helps one to put daily things in perspective and to see them in a different light. For seven years, Ansel was responsible for the international expansion of the French luxury bakery chain, Fauchon, opening stores in Russia, Egypt and Kuwait. Later on, he had the opportunity to work for six years as executive pastry chef at Daniel, one of the very top restaurants in NYC. At Daniel, Ansel was given great autonomy and this allowed him to greatly develop his skills and creative reach. But he still had more to offer...

At Dominique Ansel Bakery, the eponymous vehicle for the unfettered expression of his creative vision, Ansel had worked for two months on at least ten recipes before he was completely ready to introduce the Cronut™ to the public. This world/historical moment occurred on May 10, 2013 and since then the Cronut has certainly become perhaps the most talked about and copied dessert in the recent history of baking. (Ansel was incidentally proclaimed the "Outstanding Pastry Chef" by the James Beard Foundation in 2014.)

The Cronut is a fusion of the croissant and donut, but it would be an insult to compare this noble creation to a normal croissant or a typical donut. The secret is in the complex proportions of dough utilized and in the fact that it is fried in grape seed oil at a very precise temperature. The Cronut is then carefully rolled in sugar, filled with cream and topped with glaze. The taste changes every month, because Ansel always adapts it to the season. The entire process takes three days and is prepared completely in-house.

The result is a donut that looks like a piece of *viennoiserie*, which you should really eat right away. The inner part is spectacular because of the perfect layers of dough. If you want to cut it (naturally with a serrated knife), it is important not to destroy the layers because they are an essential part of the taste and texture experience.

But how in heaven's name do you get close enough to these delicacies that sometimes fetch up to $100 on the black market? Getting hold of a Cronut is not just a matter of impulse when you have the genial idea of surprising your loved one. You need some serious preparation. Every Monday morning before 11 o'clock, you can place an order via www.cronutpreorder.com for delivery two weeks later! For example, on Monday the 30th of June you can reserve your Cronut for any day during the week between the 14th and 20th of July, with a maximum of five Cronuts per person.

But... the early bird catches the worm. Another way of obtaining a Cronut is to stand in line – like seeking tickets to a Rolling Stones concert – as early as possible before opening hours. The bakery opens at 8:00 or 9:00 a.m. and even at these early hours you will find a long line outside. Yet it's worthwhile; just imagine the look on the face of your dearest when you come home with Cronuts!

A super talent like Ansel of course has much more to offer than just the phenomenal Cronut. His version of French classics such as cannelé and the Paris-Brest (which he calls Paris-NYC) and his blanc-manger are just as delicious. I am totally in love with his madeleines, which are baked when you order them and arrive wonderfully fresh and tasty to your plate. The Cronut is awesome, unbelievably tasty! According to *Time Magazine* this was one of the top inventions of 2013. Believe me, this is really one of the few things that makes waiting in line worthwhile.

LA BONBONNIÈRE

28 8th Ave. (between Jane and W 12th St.) - NY 10014
T (212) 741-9266

Daily 8:00 a.m. - 6:00 p.m.

A few steps away from super cool Hudson Street you will find La Bonbonnière,
a gem of the die-hard breed of diners.

Fluffy Banana pancakes

It even belongs in a rare category: the hole-in-the-wall diner, because it is certainly not big. In spite of its somewhat chic French name, it is a 100% American diner, though it would not snatch too many prizes for its interior design.

The drab brown walls attest to the fact that they have not been painted since NYC became a smoke-free city, and that was easily twenty years ago. However, this does not keep a cluster of fans from swearing by this honky-tonk diner, which is especially popular for breakfast and brunch.

La Bonbonnière does, however, possess a great deal of incredible charm in spite of the Formica counter and plastic chairs. Historically, such places have always attracted celebrities precisely because they can maintain their anonymity in such environments. In La Bonbonnière a celebrity will be less noticeable than at The Standard, for example, because here everyone is busy with themselves and not with their surroundings. From the hall of fame, I did recognize the late James Gandolfini and Ethan Hawke as habitués of the diner. It is really a place that gets to you, and whenever I see the signed CD covers hanging on the wall with titles such as Mike Viola's *The Candy Butchers, Live at La Bonbonnière*, I am endlessly impressed.

I am not actually a great fan of pancakes, but for their fluffy banana pancakes, I make a special exception. They are preternaturally fluffy and light, apparently due to the use of well-beaten buttermilk in the batter. The banana purée in the batter and extra slices of fried banana make this dish a uniquely tasteful experience, even for someone who is not crazy about pancakes.

KUTSHER'S

186 Franklin St. (Hudson and Greenwich St.) - NY 10013
T (212) 431-0606 - www.kutsherstribeca.com
Mon-Fri: 12:00-15:30, Sat-Sun: 11:00-16:00, Tues-Thurs: 17:30-21:30, Fri-Sat: 17:30-22:00

A Reuben is probably
one of the most popular sandwiches in the US.

Reuben spring rolls

A traditional version consists of thick slices of corned beef, sauerkraut, cheese slices and Thousand Island or Russian dressing. All this is stacked between two slices of rye bread and then toasted, a guilty pleasure, if not a real treat.

As with all classic dishes, its origins are highly disputed. In one version, Reuben Kulakofsky, a Lithuanian grocer from Omaha, Nebraska, is said to have invented this sandwich for his weekly poker game with friends in the Blackstone Hotel between 1920 and 1935. The hotel owner and fellow poker player, Charles Schimmel, placed it on the hotel's lunch menu and won a national competition with it. Or perhaps it was Arnold Reuben, the German owner of Reuben's Delicatessen, a once well-known deli in NYC? He had a Reuben special on his menu around 1914.

In any case, the Reuben is a fantastic sandwich that always reminds me of NYC. I don't know why... A minor drawback is that a Reuben is also a stomach-filling meal, and cruising NYC, one must always retain the slightly hungry edge. I am very thankful to Chef Jose Sanchez of Kutsher's for his Reuben spring rolls, which provide you with the taste sensation of a Reuben, but not with the feeling that you cannot eat anything else for the next few days.

This modern Jewish-American bistro offers a light, elegant, gracious, modern version of the Jewish kitchen; the dishes are easier to digest, enabling you still try a number of the other items. Since 1907, Kutsher's Country Club has been one of the iconic clubs in the fashionable Catskill Mountains region, a lovely area some 90 miles northwest of NYC. The exceptionally lively triangle under Canal Street, Tribeca, is dotted with lovely shops, beautiful people and of course good restaurants. The lovely Kutsher's is an enthralling restaurant, presenting a great opportunity to indulge in nostalgia, owing to its classic '50s interior.

REDFARM

529 Hudson St. (between W. 10th and Charles St.) - NY 10014
2170 Broadway (between W. 76th and W 77th St.) - NY 10023
T (212) 724 9700 - www.redfarmnyc.com
Mon-Sat: 5:00 p.m. -11:00 p.m., Sun: 11:00 a.m. - 2:30 p.m. and 5:00 p.m. - 11:45 p.m.

RedFarm is truly custom-made for the super cool Hudson Street.
Designer Jun Aizaki knew exactly how to make the owners' wishes come true
in this magnificent 1828 townhouse.

Pac Man shrimp dumplings

It has a pleasant balance between large group tables and small intimate spots where you can sit with one or two people or in small groups.

Joe Ng is a dim sum chef with lots of Kowloon and Hong Kong experience and has a repertoire of more than one thousand of these taste explosions. Ed Schoenfeld has prepared New Yorkers – in an almost missionary approach – for the better Chinese kitchens. This includes the fantastic Shun Lee Palace. Together this is the team of the Red-Farm. Ed was immediately convinced of the super talent of Joe Ng, and wanted to give him every opportunity to excel. Joe's aim is to create culinary delights that will even surprise himself.

Joe Ng offers a refreshing look at a number of classics from the Chinese kitchen and he fully comes alive with his very frivolous dim sums. The mushroom and vegetable spring rolls for example look like actual mushrooms and his exquisite ha kau is in the form of a potato tempura Pac chasing Blinky, Pinky, Inky and Clyde. The chicken salad is a sculptural feat and the vegetable salad seems to resemble a vegetable garden.

I truly consider RedFarm one of the very best up-market Chinese restaurants in the city. It really makes the point that one can achieve far better results by making traditional dishes with top-quality ingredients. I believe that RedFarm is the only Chinese restaurant that uses beef from the world-famous butcher, Pat LaFrieda, and I have to dig deep into my memory to come up with a better version of shrimp-stuffed chicken.

In what used to be a Laundromat, RedFarm has recently opened on its ground floor a lovely bar, Decoy, serving Chinese cuisine based on the finger food concept. Joe and Ed are a real dream team and their food definitely belongs in the higher echelons of Chinese food in NYC.

BALTHAZAR

80 Spring Street (@ Crosby Street) - NY 10012
T (212) 965-1414 - www.balthazarny.com
Mon-Fri: 7:30 a.m. - 5:00 p.m., Sat-Sun: 8:00 a.m. - 4:00 p.m., Mon-Thurs: 6:00 p.m. - midnight,
Fri-Sat: 6:00 p.m. - 1:00 a.m., Sun: 5:30 p.m. - midnight

One of the most impressive NY restaurants for me is Balthazar.
The place is always packed; that means a kind of cozy chaos.
Yet the dedication and professionalism displayed here in all areas is truly astounding.

Steak tartare

Shane transforms this seemingly simple dish into a dish of global allure

You feel immediately as if you are in one of the nicest brasseries in Paris, yet served by friendly staff!

It starts with the small bakery next to the restaurant; a small bakery, yet a great one. Just looking through the store window, you are overwhelmed by a feeling of nostalgia and appetite. Feel like having fantastic bread and *viennoiserie*? The brasserie itself is impressive and dynamic, with a menu that changes several times per day. In the evening it seems as if you are looking at a menu in France; the font and colors are selected with the same precision that a choreographer will compose for his or her best dancers. Yup, I am an unconditional fan. There was a time when I used to come here only on Sundays with friends for an extensive brunch or just to read the weekend edition of *The New York Times*, or more plausibly, skim through it, because no one can read it through completely before finishing one's eggs Benedict or sunny-side-up with the homemade blood sausage.

That is why I would like to thank my friends, Olivier and Veerle for making me aware of the marvelous steak tartare. They were both utterly enthusiastic about it and I, of course, became an instant candidate for initiation into this mystical cult. The steak tartare was even tastier than they had described it. Filet americain préparé, known locally as steak tartare, is consumed worldwide. In most places it is briefly marinated beef or horsemeat with as little fat as possible, because raw fat is just not tasty and has a less than pleasant mouth feel.

The version we are familiar with emerged at the beginning of the 20th century in restaurants in Paris in the form of steak à l'américain, made with egg yolk. The dish made culinary history in 1921 when the famous Escoffier included it in his cooking book, *Le Guide Culinaire*. For the purist – there is no inclusion of raw egg yolk – Escoffier was obstinate. In the Larousse Gastronomique of 1938, however, Escoffier's version was adapted and raw egg yolk was insinuated into the preparation.

Shane McBride, the executive chef of this unique restaurant, prepares a version of steak tartare that makes it a foremost reason to come to NYC. The quality of the meat combined with the condiments is a genuine revelation. The brilliance of the seasoning transforms this seemingly simple dish into one of global allure. Because the menu at Balthazar changes several times per day, I always feel like sitting there for hours and ordering something different from each menu. Looks to me like a nice adventure – a day trip to Balthazar, possibly remaining there forever.

CHINA BLUE

135 Watts St. (or 451 Washington St.) - NY 10013
T (212) 431-0111 - www.chinabluenewyork.com
Sun-Wed: 11:30 a.m. -11:00 p.m., Thurs-Sat: 11:30 a.m. - 11:30 p.m.

China Blue is one of these restaurants where, after eating,
you step outside and think "Everything here is just right!"

finely cut crispy eel, delicately caramelized, sprinkled with sesame seeds

Crispy eel Wuxi style

It is the brainchild of Yiming Wang, a stylish young woman who has a lot to offer. She not only has a fine taste in food, but she designs her own clothing and apparently does it quite well. In addition, she clearly has a refined sense for interior design, having designed the restaurant herself.

The atmosphere evokes the elegance and distinctness of Shanghai during the period between the two wars. The restaurant radiates classiness and you feel yourself important as soon as you enter. Somehow, this fortunately does not create a particularly onerous feeling of self-consciousness. Antique lamps, used books and old typewriters make for a very special cozy atmosphere. The music, incidence of light, the open space, seem as functional as the space that is used, and of course the fantastic food served here, completes it all.

Chef Li is the salt of the earth and he is very proud of his specialties from Shanghai. Subtlety is the mantra of this kitchen. Also his dim sum chef is a real magician/craftsman. In my opinion, what comes out of this dim sum kitchen has no rival in NY, neither in the realm of authenticity nor in its precision and presentation. A commanding dish that the entire city should taste is the so very typical Xiaolongbao, the ultimate signature Shanghai dumpling and the pumpkin cakes filled with red beans. Choosing a Must Eat here is once again a thankless task, because the number of unforgettable dishes here is countless. For example, I was knocked off my feet by the slow-cooked lion's head meatball, and the eight delicacies in spicy sauce, just to name a few. All the same, I would definitely go for the crispy eel Wuxi style. The finely cut eel is crispy and crunchy and very delicately caramelized, and then sprinkled with roasted sesame seeds. This dish has it all, a complex play of hearty and sweet.

Shanghai cuisine, also known as Hu, is quite popular, closely resembling the cuisine of the surrounding provinces of Jiangsu and Zhejiang. The Chinese sometimes talk about Benbang cuisine when referring to these three. Typical of this cuisine is the use of alcohol, wine, fish and crab. Preserved vegetables and salted meat are often used for flavoring, and sugar and soy sauce are also popular combinations.

MARINA VERA LUZ

Near the La Senora de Guadeloupe church
328 W 14th St. (between 8th and 9th Avenue) - NY 10014
Daily 6:00 a.m. - 3:00 p.m.

I very much admire the street vendors
who get up early every day and defy the weather gods.

her assortment varies depening on
her mood and shopping but tamales and pozole
are always available

Mexican street food

Marina Vera Luz is additionally a very devout woman, because every Sunday she stands in front of the church of her Mexican holy patroness, La Señora de Guadeloupe. That church has five masses each Sunday, but the real traffic is at her food stand in the shadow of the church. At 2 o'clock in the morning her alarm clock goes off and everything that she prepared the evening before together with a girlfriend is loaded to the van. East Harlem, where she has been living with her husband Moises and her family since 1987, is left behind for Chelsea.

Customers are sometimes waiting even *before* everything is unloaded, and that is understandable. Waiting by the church are not only churchgoers, but also cabbies, firemen and the occasional tourist who finds his hotel's breakfast buffet inedible. In my opinion, Marina's food is the best Mexican food that you will find in NYC. It is made from the heart, and of course based on family recipes. Her assortment varies a bit depending on her mood and shopping, but tamales and pozole are always available.

Tamales are a traditional Mexican breakfast dish and Marina's version tastes the best. It is deceptively very simple, but that is where the complexity arises. Corn dough is filled with meat, vegetables, cheese, fruit or rice and then rolled and steamed. The tamale is such an old recipe that its origin has long been forgotten. It was described in 1569 by the Spanish missionary Bernardino de Sahagun in his famous book, *Historia General de las Cosas de la Nueva España*. He also described the traditional pre-Columbian soup or pozole stew. The basis for this is nixtamal corn, steamed with meat, chili peppers and other tasty ingredients. If she has mole poblano at her stand, you must definitely try her version; one of the world's best recipes. These are chicken drumsticks steamed in a complex mixture of chicken broth, various types of chili peppers, aromatic herbs, old bread, nuts and cacao. The first time this dish was prepared was when the nuns of the Santa Rosa cloister in Puebla de Los Angeles panicked, because the archbishop came for a visit and they had nothing to serve at the table. The chicken in this deep, dark sauce turned out to be incredibly delicious. Marina has never skipped a Sunday.

BABBO

110 Waverly Place (between Washington Square West and Avenue of the Americas) - NY 10011
T (212) 777-0303 - www.babbonyc.com
Mon: 5:30 p.m. - 11:00 p.m., Tues-Sat: 11:30 a.m. - 11:00 p.m., Sun: 4:30 p.m. - 10:30 p.m.

The best Italian restaurant in NY
is not located in Little Italy.

Beef cheek ravioli, pigeon liver and black truffles

To enjoy the best Italian food, you have to go to Babbo, the crown of the restaurant empire of the phenomenal chef, author and media star, Mario Batali. He is also an expert in the history and culture of the Italian kitchen, specializing (if one can say that about someone as peripatetic as Mario) in all the regional and local varieties. He is a co-owner of twenty-one restaurants and the author of nine cookbooks.

The grandfather of Molto Mario, as he is sometimes called, left Abruzzo in 1899 to work in the copper mines in Butte, Montana, but later move on to Seattle, where Mario was born in 1960. By now, Batali is a co-owner of various restaurants around the world, but his favorite no doubt is Babbo, which he opened together with Joseph Bastianich.

This place commends the best tradition in Italian hospitality and offers the most exemplary features of Italian cuisine. Their philosophy is simple and straightforward: use only the best local ingredients and serve them as simply as possible. Just as a native of Naples would cook on the Amalfi coast, the cooks at Babbo cook like an Italian on the Mid-Atlantic coast or Hudson Valley. Like most Italian chefs, they love where they live and their kitchen celebrates both their location and their ingredients from the land *and* sea. Babbo is their interpretation of Batali's personal philosophy.

At Babbo you will rarely find your favorite regional classics as you have eaten them in tiny osterias throughout Italy. For me, the menu is a sort of entry ticket into Italian heaven. Batali's versions of Italian *osteria* dishes are sometimes even better that what I remember from Italy. Moreover, the music here is far better than in most Italian restaurants. What always enchants me is the lightness of these seemingly powerful dishes. I only have to think back to the tortellini with goat cheese, sprinkled with dried orange and wild fennel seeds to taste it once again, and this goes just as much for the *brasato al Barolo* (beef braised in Barolo wine), which tastes just slightly better than the version I ate in Brà, at Boccondivino.

Babbo is a phenomenon; the dream of any Italophile and simply a must for every connoisseur of fantastic food and drinks. The wine list by the way is also 100% Italian. Every time I come here, I can think of only one thing: What excuse can I find for coming back here as soon as possible? Forza Mario Batali!

RAMEN.CO BY KEIZO SHIMAMOTO

100 Maiden Ln - NY 10038
T (646) 490-8456 - www.ramen.co
Open Mon-Fri: 11:00 a.m. - 9:00 p.m.

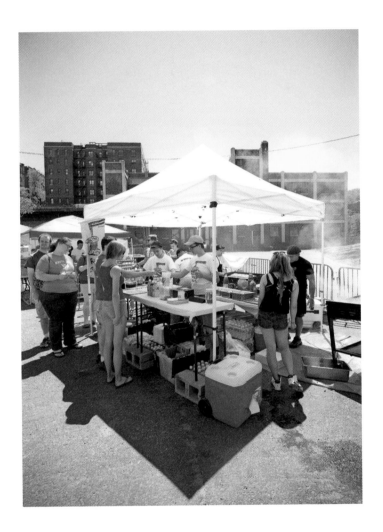

When Keizo Shimamoto traveled around Japan in order to study ramen,
he missed NYC very much and had serious yearnings for ... hamburgers.

an insane idea!

Ramen burger

As a Japanese, this was a totally unexpected experience of culture shock. His brain, driven by homesickness, gave him the impetus for what was to become an insane idea: the Ramen Burger.

With fear in his heart, he presented his idea to the public for the first time in June 2013 at the Smorgasburg festival in Brooklyn. An insane hype was born. The ramen burger was the perfect blend of Japanese and American cultures on the one hand, and two of Keizo's best childhood memories on the other – hamburgers and ramen. The ramen burger in all its varieties is surprising, mischievous, challenging, tasty, confusing. It is naturally not everyone's lot to have an idea, to implement it and see it grow into a phenomenon, as was the case with the ramen burger.

Keizo makes four variations of ramen burgers and they have only one thing in common: there is no bun. The bun is replaced by two perfectly cooked, bun-shaped ramen noodles, held in place by pressing them together and baking them. In between a fantastic Angus beef burger is a bit of arugula, a slice of cheddar, a lovely soy sauce glazing prepared by Keizo and freshly chopped scallions. The other variations are yakitori instead of beef, unraveled beef and tofu.

NYC is now completely subjugated by the ramen burger;, Los Angeles and Hawaii are currently being targeted. There are various new locations in the offing (currently you can only eat a ramen burger at ramen.co and at Smorgasburg) in order to meet the hysterical demand. Recently, BERG'N was opened: a new Beer Garten (899 Bergen Street in Brooklyn, NY 11238) where the ramen burger is always on the menu. Honolulu and LA are next. Stay tuned; it is not inconceivable you will soon see ramen fries!

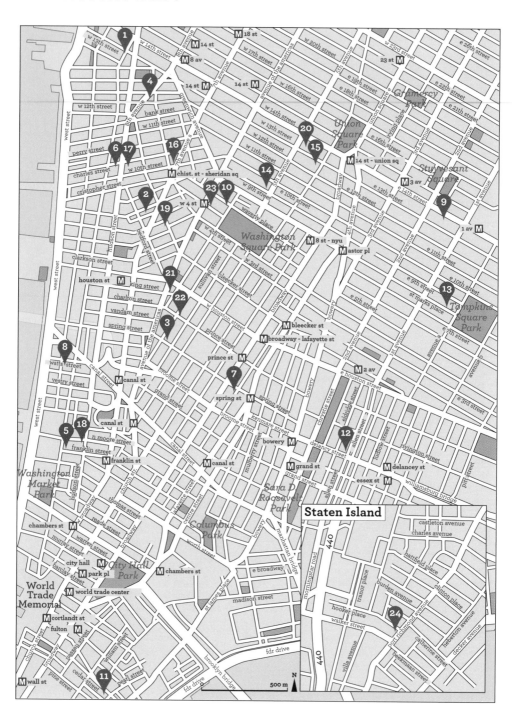

ADDITIONAL EATERIES

12 BENKEI RAMEN
115 Allen Street, NY 10002
T +1 201 290 8682
www.benkeiramenusa.com
▸ **Tonkatsu ramen**

13 BOX KITE NYC
115 St Marks Place (between 1st and A), NY 10009
T +1 212 574 820
www.boxkitenyc.com
▸ **Coffee shop with a secret tasting menu**

14 CLAUDETTE
24 Fifth Avenue (9th Street), NY 10011
T +1 212 868 2424
www.claudettenyc.com
▸ **Bouillabaise en croûte**

15 ALL'ONDA
22 E 13th Street, NY 10003
T +1 212 231 2236
www.allondanyc.com
▸ **Bucatini, smoked uni, spicy bread crumbs**

16 CHEZ SARDINE
183 West 10th Street, NY 10014
T +1 646.360.3705
www.chezsardine.com
▸ **Foie gras and smoked cheddar grilled cheese sandwich**

17 DECOY
529-1/2 Hudson Street (downstairs), NY 10014
T +1 212 792 9700
www.decoynyc.com
▸ **Peking duck feast**

18 NOBU
105 Hudson Street (Franklin Street), NY 10013
T +1 212 219 0500
www.noburestaurants.com/new-york
▸ **Uni tempura**

19 MURRAY'S CHEESE BAR
264 Bleecker Street (between Morton Street and Leroy Street), NY 10014
T +1 646 476 8882
www.murrayscheesebar.com
▸ **Seasonal cheesemongers flight**

20 CORKBUZZ WINE STUDIO
13 E 13th Street, (between University Place and 5th Avenue), NY 10003
T +1 646 873 6071
www.corkbuzz.com
▸ **Lardo wrapped quail, charred scallion, mint, citrus salad**

21 CHARLIE BIRD
5 King Street (6th Avenue), NY 10012
T +1 212 235 7133
www.charliebirdnyc.com
▸ **Grilled octopus saltimbocca, ceci beans, sage & prosciutto di Parma**

22 THE DUTCH
131 Sullivan Street (Prince Street), NY 10012
T +1 212 677 6200
www.thedutchnyc.com
▸ **Cajun quail, dirty rice shrimp stuffing**

23 BLUE HILL
75 Washington Place (between McDougall and 6th), NY 10011
T +1 212 539 1776
www.bluehillfarm.com/food/blue-hill-new-york
▸ **Daily menu and tasting**

24 DENINO'S
524 Port Richmond Avenue (between Hooker Place and Walker Street) - NY 10302 (Staten Island)
T +1 718 442 9401
www.deninos.com
▸ **Garbage pie pizza**

KATZ'S DELICATESSEN

205 E Houston St. - NY 10002
T (212) 254-2246 - www.katzdelicatessen.com

Open Mon-Wed: 8:00 a.m. - 10:45 p.m., Thurs: 8:00 a.m. - 2:45 a.m., Fri: 8:00 - open all night, Sat: open the entire day! Sun: until 10:45 p.m.

Pastrami is like a journey in time. The term signifies an age-old method
of preserving meat by pickling, drying it slightly, mixing it with various herbs
and then slowly smoking and steaming it.

Pastrami on rye sandwich

Pastrami's origins are not entirely clear. It might have originated in Turkey where it was called pastirma or perhaps in Romania where pastra means 'to store'. We will never be quite sure. What is for certain is that the first pastrami sandwiches in NY emerged during the wave of Jewish immigration from Romania and Bessarabia. In Yiddish it was called pastrome, which evolved into pastrama in English and later, analogous to salami, it became pastrami.

Sussman Volk, a kosher butcher, received a pastrami recipe from a Romanian friend and made the first pastrami sandwich in 1887. This became so popular that his butcher's shop had to make way for a restaurant. In 1888, the Iceland brothers opened a small deli on the corner of Ludlow Street and E. Houston called 'Iceland Brothers'. When they entered a partnership with Willy Katz in 1903, the name was changed to Iceland & Katz.

In 1917, it moved to the other side of the street where it is still located to this day. Benny Katz later bought out the Iceland brothers and he is now the one who keeps Katz's cruising along.

Katz's Delicatessen is one of the greatest culinary shrines in NY. It is an institution that lives up to its reputation, time and again. Even though it resembles a football refectory, I can't keep away from this place. It has something magical and enticing for both tourists and locals. The pastrami sandwich is a gastronomical monument, a benchmark, a lodestone for all other pastrami sandwiches in the world. The taste, the texture, the seasoning, all pure perfection, and a sandwich for everyone's bucket list. It should not be forgotten that Meg Ryan experienced her revelatory/orgasmic moment at Katz's in the movie *When Harry Met Sally*. I recommend that you have whatever (no doubt it was the pastrami) she was having.

PLEASE KEEP HANDS
OUT OF BARRELS

THE PICKLE GUYS

TASTES BETTER!!

The Pickle Guys

THE PICKLE GUYS

49 Essex St. - NY 10002
T (212) 656-9739 - www.pickleguys.com
Open Sun-Thurs: 9:00 a.m. - 6:00 p.m., Fri: 9:00 a.m. - 4:00 p.m.

Essex Street, in the Lower East Side, has always been the pickle center of NY. As far back as 1910, there have always been numerous traditional pickle makers on Essex Street.

Pickles

But, alas, at this moment, this establishment is perhaps the last place in NY where you can buy and eat all sorts of traditionally preserved fruits and vegetables. The history of pickling is very old; the discovery of pickling and preserving is probably one of the most important phenomena in man's cultural evolution. When inhabitants of north India brought cucumbers and cucumber seeds to Mesopotamia (and we are talking of around 2030 BCE), pickling and preserving was discovered.

Pickles are mentioned at least twice in the Bible; the ancient Egyptians were familiar with them, and the Romans always brought home lots of food from the regions that they conquered, usually preserved in vinegar, oil, brine, sometimes in honey, and sometimes in garum (or liquamen), actually a leakage fluid from fermented, salted fish, usually anchovy. Nowadays, this is known as *colatura di alici* and is considered a delicacy. The English word "pickle" (don't confuse it with piccalilli) emerged in the language for the first time around 1400 CE and it means a spicy sauce to eat with meat and fowl. In Dutch the word *pekel* (brine) shares the same etymological origins. Throughout history, Jews have always preserved many fruits and vegetables; Ashkenazi Jews have continued the tradition of preserving in wooden barrels or ceramic pots.

I have always admired young people who make an effort to breathe new life into nearly forgotten traditions. And this is what they are doing here, with passion and dedication. Never before have I tasted more delicious preserved food. Here too, we see an unparalleled balance in the products themselves. Not too sour, not too salty, these are pickles and preserves made with great precision. In a time when everything is industrialized, the sight of a 100% artisanal shop is a true relief. Barrels containing pickled delicacies are displayed in this simple store where tasting is allowed, touching is not, of course. No magic tricks here with preservative agents; what you see is what you get! The recipes come from Alan Kaufmann's mother and have remained absolutely unchanged. Unique is the preserved watermelon, as well as preserved mango, garlic, okra, mushrooms and much more. These tastes cannot be compared to anything you have ever had before. Furthermore, everything is kosher, as the shop is under the strict rabbinical supervision of Rabbi Shmuel Fisheli. For the devotees of the slightly arcane, the owners recently started to make Russel (or sour) Borscht, a wonderful, traditional beet soup made of preserved beets.

Live GeoDuck Clam
新鮮象拔蚌

ORIENTAL GARDEN

14 Elisabeth St. (between Canal and Bayard St.) - NY 10013
T (212) 619-0085 - www.orientalgardennyc.com
Open Mon-Fri: 10:00 a.m. - 10:30 p.m., Sat-Sun: 9:00 a.m. - 11:00 p.m.

In NYC's vast Chinatown it is not always so easy
to separate the wheat from the chaff.

*they work genuine magic
with live Geoduck*

Raw sliced geoduck

Every place has its specialty and in this restaurant it is most definitely fish and seafood. To make the point clear, this unique Cantonese restaurant features numerous aquariums at its entrance, insuring that all of its delicious offerings are as fresh as they can be.

Another special feature of the restaurant is the separate cooler where the more unique and currently available seafood is displayed: hand-dived scallops, large, wild, shucked oysters; live jumbo shrimps and – an item that will catch your attention if available – the giant clam, also called the geoduck or mirugai. This bivalve shellfish is a unique creature, one of the most long-living species on earth; an existence of 150 years is not exceptional. The rather strange name comes from Lushootseed, from an old Indian dialect of the tribes that formerly inhabited Washington State. It means 'dig deep' and this shellfish actually digs itself deep into the sand while only its siphon, which can be up to one meter long, protrudes. Although considered a delicacy in many places, amazingly, it has only been commercially cultivated from around 1970.

Among all the other top dishes in their repertoire, the Oriental Garden team really seems to work genuine magic with the geoduck. I prefer to eat it raw, in thin slices, rather like the Japanese would prepare sashimi. The meat of the siphon has a very strong taste of the sea and a special texture; the harder pieces are lightly floured and served after being rapidly deep-fried at a high temperature. These two preparation methods bring out the purity of this remarkable seafood and demonstrate the chef's respect for this unusual produce. Oriental Garden is a grand kitchen in all its tranquility and unpretentiousness.

YONAH SCHIMMEL

137 E Houston St. (between 1st and 2nd Ave.) - NY 10002
T (212) 477-2858- www.knishery.com
Open Sun - Thurs 9 a.m. - 7:30 p.m., Fri - Sat: 9 a.m. - 11 p.m.

A knish (or knysh) is a traditional snack/meal
that was very popular mainly in Eastern Europe.

Potato knish

walk in and have a taste of NYC history

Like many of these types of snacks, they are prepared in different shapes and with a wide variety of fillings. Most knishes are filled with mashed potatoes mixed with minced meat, sauerkraut, onions or cabbage. Kasha, as a filling, was enormously popular in the Jewish Ashkenazi community. They are round, square or rectangular in shape and their size varies depending on whether you eat the knish as a snack or a meal. In cities with a large Jewish population you often still see street vendors selling delicious knishes.

Around 1890, Yonah Schimmel, a Romanian immigrant, began to sell his knishes made from a family recipe. His next logical step was to open a store, and

he did that on Houston Street together with his nephew Joseph Berger, becoming the first knish maker in NYC in 1910. Yonah left the business a few years later and Joseph stayed on. The neighborhood has definitely changed in the intervening years; much of the Jewish population has moved out of the Lower East Side, but the little store and the knishes remain unchanged. This authentic neighborhood store is such a NY landmark that we find it in the Woody Allen movie, *Whatever Works*, and in a 1929 painting by Hedgy Pagremanski, which can be viewed in the permanent collection of the Museum of the City of New York. The next time you are strolling past this bakery, walk in and taste a piece of NY history.

Lam Zhou Hand Made Noodle & Dumpl

牛肉拉麵
Beef Soup Noodle

豬肉拉麵
Pork Soup Noodle

羊肉拉麵
Soup Noodle With Lamb

鴨肉墨魚麵
Duck Soup Noodle

水餃　鍋貼

牛尾粉干
Ox Tail Soup With Rice Noodle   22. 6.00
牛飛化
Beef Tripe With thin Rice Noodle   23. 5.50
排骨线面
Steam Pork Soup With Fuzhou Flour Vermicelli 24. 5.50
煎蛋
Fried Egg.   25. 1+/0.5
北发冰涷汤圆. 元宵
Frozen Sweet Ot Salt rice ball. (50p) 26. 12.50
本楼刀削面
House special knife cut soup noodle 27. 7.50.

LAM ZHOU

East Broadway (between Pike and Rutgers St.) - NY 10002
T (212) 566-6933

Open Mon-Sun: 10:30 a.m.- 11:00 p.m.

One of the first things I try to do when I am in Southeast Asia
is to have a bowl of hearty noodle soup at one of the countless noodle shops.

House special hand-cut noodle soup

the perfect bowl of noodle soup exists

This gives me a kind of homey feeling; it is a kind of "Welcome to Asia", disguised as a bowl of soup.

The basic ingredients are broth, noodles, a few fresh vegetables, a bit of fish and/or meat and a few spices. It seems so simple, but the fact that outside of Asia this delicious, steamed noodle soup rarely evokes the same wonderful feeling and flavorful sensation convinces me more and more that we simply do not take this delicacy seriously enough.

This is far from the case at Lam Zhou. The interior is non-existent, as is the décor. Everything here points only to the essential: the food! East Broadway is perhaps not the most aesthetically harmonious street but you should not be misled by the look of a restaurant.

Lam Zhou is highly patronized by the Chinese population and a few intimate friends, and it is certainly the kitchen that has merited this attention in virtue of its no-nonsense policy.

The kitchen prepares fresh noodles that are used in an assortment of dishes, mostly in soups or in woks with various garnishes. Believe me, all of these creations are excellent. For the handmade noodles, the portions are chipped off from a thick block of pasta into small, irregular pieces that are processed further. The broth is extremely rich in taste. The handmade noodles offer lots of diversity, considering that they come in a multitude of sizes and thickness. The garnishing of the soups provides a wide variety of genuine taste explosions. A perfect fried egg fully completes the dish. The perfect noodle soup exists!

腸粉	大L	$5.00	爽口魚蛋	$1.00
Rice Noodles	中M	$2.50	Fish Balls	6粒
	小S	$1.75	正宗咸肉粽	$1.50
腸粉魚蛋	大L	$6.50	Glutious Rice	
Rice Noodles & Fish Balls	中M	$3.00	珍珠雞	$1.25
	小S	$2.00	Glutinous Rice in Lotus Leaf	
茶葉蛋		$1.25	炒撈麵	$1.50
Tea Eggs		3只	Lo Mein	
精制牛肚		$5.50	炒米粉	$1.50
Tripe			Mai Fun	
腸粉牛肚		$3.25	皮蛋瘦肉粥	$2.50
Rice Noodles & Tripe			Congee with Minced Pork & Preserved Eggs	$1.50

Extra sauce per order ＊ add 25¢

多醬 每一份 加 25¢

RUTGER STREET FOOD CART

Corner of East Broadway-Rutger St. - NY 10002

Open daily 6:00 a.m. - 4:00 p.m.

There are many small, mobile eating stalls in Chinatown. They all offer their own specialties but to the best of my knowledge only one of them offers tea eggs.

Tea eggs

the ideal insider snack

Tea eggs are very popular snacks in China and in cities with a large Chinese community. The delicately perfumed, lovely marbled eggs are mostly a feast for the eye, but they are also truly delicious. The idea is actually quite simple. Eggs are hard-boiled and then, with the help of a spoon, randomly cracked into a bowl. The smaller and finer the cracks in the egg, the prettier the end result. After cracking the eggs in the bowl, they are cooked again in a mixture of strong tea, five spices, cinnamon, soy sauce, star anise, fennel seeds, Szechuan peppercorns and cloves. The eggs are heated for another 30 minutes and afterwards remain for a few days in this marinade, obviously having cooled. When you then peel the eggs, the result is exceedingly pretty: the Platonic egg, imbued with heady tea and spice, as well as the very subtle flavor of the marinade. The ideal insider snack.

INDESSERT

1 E Broadway (between Catherine St. and Chatham Square) - NY 10038
T (212) 528-3188 - www.facebook.com/Indessert
Open Sun-Thurs: Noon - 11:00 p.m., Fri-Sat: Noon - Midnight

Together with Joe Ngai from Hong Kong, Young Mei Dan Huang
runs a business in Chinatown that really stands out.

completely inundated by mango

Mango pomelo sago soup

They serve Cantonese desserts in a modern form, but still according to age-old tradition. Their store also looks rather different than all the others; a well-lighted place that is also very clean and neat. In Chinatown, where you can find almost anything, there are, oddly enough, no dessert restaurants like this. Mei specializes in Tong Sui, desserts from Canton.

Sago is a type of sweet soup based on sago (large tapioca pearls), milk, coconut milk and in this case, beautiful ripe mangos. The taste is surprisingly strong, as you are completely overwhelmed by the mango. Pomelo ensures a balance to the entirety. Be sure to taste the restaurant's specialty desserts based on black sesame. I have tasted black sesame desserts from Brussels to Hong Kong, but rarely have I seen such precision as you find in this dessert house in Chinatown NYC. Also worth trying is the Black Sesame Tong Yuen (a rich rice ball filled with almost liquid black sesame paste), but fasten your seatbelts because you will be experiencing one of the sexiest desserts you'll ever encounter.

TAQUITORIA

168 Ludlow St. (between E Houston and Stanton St.) - NY 10002
T (212) 780-0121 - www.taquitoria.com
Open Tues-Sun: 4:00 p.m.- 2:00 a.m.

A taquito or flauta is a tortilla tightly rolled
around a filling and then deep-fried.

Flauta, chronic style

this team rescued the taquito
from public obliquy

It is an incredibly popular snack, although in its most commonly found form, it might well be considered by sensitive palates as borderline inedible. While most snacks have by now been restyled and served in places where you can actually take your date, this has not been the case with the taquito. It has tended to languish away in heat-retaining hot dog receptacles in local supermarkets – a rather dismal fate. Until now, that is, when the team behind Taquitoria decided to rescue the taquito from public obloquy.

There are three essential elements in this snack: the tortilla, the filling and the sauce. The tortilla must be particularly crispy and with the system that they have developed, that is indeed the case for up to two hours. Their 6-inch tortilla is first fried at a low temperature and afterwards, fried for a second time at a high temperature – somewhat like Belgian French fries. For the filling, only the best is good enough. BE chicken (Bell & Evans) is first salted for two hours and then broiled in Batch 22 Bloody Mary Mix of Marc Forgione: a lovely kick of wasabi and a hint of mustard. Over this goes a bit of Cholula, a top Mexican sauce from Chapala, Jalisco, a bit of salted Jalapeno relish, guacamole sauce, pancho red sauce and a hint of sour cream – and you will never forget this flauta which the owners refer to as chronic style.

Don't be misled by the graffiti-painted walls of this nice eatery. Three friends who work together at Marc Forgione raised this Taquitoria from the ground: Matthew Conway (former sommelier), Barry Frish and Brad Holtzman. They certainly make the best taquito that I have ever tasted.

LOS PERROS LOCOS

201 Allen St. (E. Houston at Stanton St. - NY 10002
T (212) 473-1200 - www.losperroslocos.com
Sun-Wed: Noon-1:00 a.m.; Thu: until 3 a.m.; Fri-Sat: until 4 a.m.

Sausage is one of the oldest forms of ready-made food that we know.
It's even mentioned in Homer's *Odyssey*.

Amerro-Perro

the coolest dog around

The frankfurter is usually associated with its eponymous birthplace, Frankfurt-am-Main. This however is contested because people believe that the Dachshund (the local name of this totally tubular treat) was created by Johann Georgehehner, a butcher from Coburg, Germany, sometime at the end of the 17th century. This butcher used to sell his goods in Frankfurt where they were extremely popular. That did not dissuade Frankfurt from celebrating 500 years of the hot dog in 1987. The Austrians, in turn, have claimed that it is Vienna that is the true birthplace of the hot dog.

Where the real truth lies we shall never know. Neither shall we ever know who first thought of the idea of placing a hot dog in a bun and presenting it in a form that made it easier to manage. It is assumed that an unknown German immigrant opened a stand in the Bowery in 1860, but it is an established fact that Charles Feltman opened the very first hot dog stand in Coney Island in 1871. During that first year he sold 3,684 Dachshund sausages! Since those early (dog) days, the hot dog has come a long way. Would Bruce Kraig, Ph.D, a retired hot dog historian have heard of Los Perros Locos? Possibly not. Alex Mitow, the founder of Los Perros Locos has added some recent data to my long view of hot dog history. Born and raised in Miami, and therefore very much inclined towards the culinary taste of Central and South America, Mitow found himself in the position of re-imagining the hot dog. One very late night, with the umpteenth 15-dollar cocktail in his hand, a hot dog covered with French Fries caught his eye and that must have crystallized his idea.

A former Chinese bakery in the Lower East Side looked like the perfect location for the renaissance of the dog – of course after restyling it in steel and neon. UR, a local street art team, gave it a complete new life with their striking graffiti.

James Van Girish, the talented chef of Los Perros Locos, makes fantastic hot dog creations which you really must eat with the popular salchipapas, a helping of different forms of French Fries. The amerro-perro is particularly sensational. The basis is of course a nice hot dog, topped with beef chili with beer and permeated with cacao, on top of that, freshly grated Cheddar cheese from Vermont, sauerkraut with chipotle, crushed fritos complete with ChipZana sauce. The coolest hot dog around!

ODESSA

119 Ave. A (between East 7th St. and St. Marks Place) - NY 10009
T (212) 253-1482 - www.odessanyc.com
Open Mon -Thurs: 8:00 a.m. - 2:45 a.m., Fri-Sun: noon - midnight

I have the impression that typical diners (the restaurants, not the people)
are a dying race in NYC. That's a pity because a diner is often the obvious place
for experiencing the soul of a city or neighborhood.

Pierogi — impossible to walk past without stepping in

At the edge of Alphabet City, on Tompkins Square Park, there is still one such diner, which I find impossible to walk past without stepping in and nibbling on their legendary pierogi. Odessa looks as if it has always been there and whenever I sit there and look around, I have the impression that it is almost part of the club scene. What I mean to say is that Odessa is used a lot by clubbers, returning from a strenuous evening of God only knows what. I especially find it a very pleasant spot for breakfast or brunch. The breakfasts are classic and very well prepared, and the service is always friendly. Like most diners, the coffee is regrettably undrinkable, yet I always seem to fall into the trap of accepting a refill.

Obviously, you cannot leave this place without eating their pierogi. Pierogi – originally a Polish word – is actually a plural. They are a type of dumpling, typically semi-circular in shape, and cooked or baked or a combination of both. They are usually rather diminutive in size, so that you need about eight pieces to assuage your hunger. This Polish national food is eaten in most of Eastern Europe and therefore comes in all sorts of variations and with different types of fillings – from hearty to sweet. I am mostly a fan of the classic filling of ground beef as well as of the dumpling made with cabbage or sauerkraut. If you are on a discovery tour, then ask for half your portion cooked and the other half fried...

ZUCKER BAKERY

433 E 9th St. (between Ave. A and 1st Ave.) - NY 10009
T (646) 559-8425 - www.zuckerbakery.com
Open Tues-Fri: 8:00 a.m. - 6:00 p.m., Sat-Sun: 9:00 a.m. - 6:00 p.m.

After a solid breakfast at Odessa, I accidentally stumbled upon this lovely, sober and cozy bakery and just had to step in.

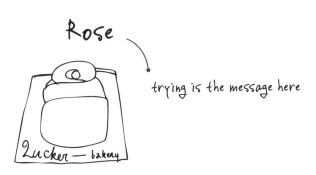

Rose

trying is the message here

Zucker — bakery

The bakery was actually hosting a Zhà pop-up, a pan-Asian street-food concept popular in NY. Their bulgogi balls were superb, but the subtle smells in this gingerbread house in the East Village made me curious to find out what else I could nibble on there.

When Zohar Zohar established this bakery, she really wanted to evoke the emotions and smells that reminded her of her grandmother's house. And she has achieved this wonderfully. Everything is baked in-house in small quantities; this is definitely the smell of freshly-baked cookies and cakes that I associate with my own grandmother's efforts. But when I really focus on these aromas, I notice that Zohar has more talent than my grandmother, because the scents here are magisterial. Zohar learned her baking skills from Daniel Boulud and David Bouley and was inspired by her colleague and friend, Johnny Iuzzini.

Her Israeli roots give this place its exotic, irresistible, Middle-Eastern feel that penetrates into the very subtle cakes (Good God, the Chocolate Babka!) and pastries. For me, the rose – closest translation would be the "sticky bun" or "cinnamon roll" is one of the most exciting pastries I have ever tasted, and exceptionally rewarding. Zohar's repertoire is truly reminiscent of her personal journey through her past and roots, whether it is the clove-flavored rugelach, the halvah with date pastry or the cardamom cookies. Trying is the message here.

OTTO'S TACOS

141 Second Ave. (between E 9th St. and St. Marks place) - NY 10003
T (646) 678-4018 - www.ottostacos.com
Open Sun-Thurs: Noon - midnight, Fri-Sat: Noon - 2:00 a.m.

Taco is not short for Taco Bell, as many youngsters might think,
but it is an old, traditional dish from Mexico – a tortilla made
of corn flour and rolled with a filling.

The gorgon

when I hear the word Gorgon my mouth begins to water

The first time that a European ate a taco was at a dinner organized by Hernan Cortés for his captains in Coyoacan around 1520.

You will notice Otto's place instantly because it is very different; it seems more like the grab-and-go taco joints that you find everywhere in Los Angeles. Although Otto Cedeno, the owner and founder, and, Joe LoNigro, the chef, are not originally from NY, they have managed to adopt the perverse tradition of many NYC restaurateurs: creating a fantastic dish and making every effort to conceal it from the public. The off-menu sensation in this joint is the gorgon. To be honest, when I hear the word gorgon, my mouth begins to water, a kind of Pavlovian reaction.

All the tortillas here are freshly made from scratch; for the gorgon – if you get the opportunity to order it – there is the extra effort. This tortilla is rolled out paper-thin and then fried. The result is a remarkable texture that comes close to that of a croissant. This tortilla is transformed into a taco by the filling of freshly-grilled, perfectly seasoned meat of your choice, homemade guacamole, serrano-chili cream, freshly chopped onions and cilantro. The combination of flavors is unique and habit-forming. Only in San Antonio is there such a thing as this puffy taco, the only one that resembles this gorgon.

Whenever I eat a gorgon (thank you Diome and Nicky), people always stare at me – at my gorgon – with hungry eyes. Take into account that only very nice people are permitted to order a gorgon.

DICKSON'S FARMSTAND

75 9th Ave. (in Chelsea Market, between 16th and 15th St.) - NY 10011
T (212) 242-2630 - www.dicksonsfarmstand.com
Open Mon-Sat: 10:00 a.m. - 8:30 p.m., Sun: 10:00 a.m. - 8:00 p.m.

Whenever I walk through Chelsea Market,
I inevitably get sucked into this top artisanal butchery.

CHARCUTERIE IS
THE DRUG THAT
I NEED TO SCORE.

Handmade
artisanal
charcuterie

Ted Rosen is a butcher with a real twinkle in his eyes as he tells you about meat and fine cold cuts, and he is even happier when he sees how you enjoy his products.

It is not easy to find artisanal charcuterie or cold cuts in NYC, and seeing that I can't go too long without it, Dickson's is an ideal refueling station. Charcuterie is the drug and I need to score. If you look closely around you, you quickly discover that this is not your run-of-the-mill butchery. It starts with entire animals. The carcasses come in one piece and are entirely chopped up by professional butchers – right in the store where everyone can follow their nimble fingers. The noblest parts are placed on the counter, the less noble parts, but usually the tastiest, are processed in the charcuterie workshop into paté, ham, coppa (cured meat), bacon, pastrami, chorizo sausages, hotdogs, rillettes and blood sausages.

All the meat sold here comes from sustainable, small-scale meat farms. These are small farms that raise traditional breeds and moreover, they don't use any antibiotics or hormones. A four-legged dream. You can come here for delicious cold-cut sandwiches or you can buy the products and eat them at home; there are fantastic cuts of pork, beef or lamb, and fowl. Top address!

NOM WAH TEA PARLOR

13 Doyers St. (between Bowery and Pell St.) - NY 10013
T (212) 962-6047 - www.nomwah.com
Open Sun-Thurs: 10:30 a.m. - 9:00 p.m., Fri-Sat: 10:30 a.m. - 10:00 p.m.

Doyers Street is a somewhat forgotten street in Chinatown, yet it has a rich history.
Hendrik Doyer, a Dutch immigrant, had a distillery here in 1791, and between 1893 and 1911
this was the location of the first Chinese theater.

The original egg roll

The slightly strange bend in the road has given it the nickname 'the bloody angle' because this street was the scene of countless shoot-outs by the Tong gangs. On no other street in the US have so many people been killed.

In 1920, the Choy family opened a Chinese bakery and tea house at number 13-15. It became famous for its mooncake filling, red bean filling and almond cookies, which are still a specialty of the house. In 1968, the lease expired and the manager, Wally Tang, who had worked there since 1950 from the age of sixteen, moved the business to number 11-13. And that is where Nom Wah Tea Parlor still stands. Wally Tang bought the place in 1974; his life work is now being carried out by his family. 'Dim, *ergo* sum.'

Dim sum is no doubt my favorite way of eating. I have always been impressed by the speed that genuine dim sum restaurants can conjure up an unbelievable variety of tastes and forms. Everyone savors and enjoys, it is supercozy and everyone is delighted.

Dim sum is not really a snack, as many people mistakenly think. It refers to a way of eating. Dim sum means literally 'stirring your heart'. In Cantonese, people refer to it as yum cha, which means 'tea drinking'. This better exposes the roots of dim sum, as it actually originates from the time of the Silk Route when many resting places were established for travelers, and where tea was served with small snacks. Many of my most heroic meals were dim sum meals: the variety, the diversity, the purity in taste sensation and especially the play on textures raises a top dim sum chef to one of the greatest culinary masters.

In my opinion, Nom Wah's dim sum is one of the best that I have ever eaten outside of China. The sui mai, the har kau, pure perfection. The egg roll is legendary and tastes insanely good. A paper-thin omelet in a tasty batter, filled with crispy stir-fried water chestnuts, Chinese celery, bean sprouts and various vegetables. A monumental dish.

AMAZING 66

66 Mott St. (between Canal St. and Bayard St.) - NY 10013
T (212) 334-0099 - www.amazing66.com
Open daily: 11:00 a.m. - 11:00 p.m.

When Reinhard Löwenstein, a good friend and a top Riesling winemaker
from the Mosel came to visit me, I took him to Chinatown and there in one of the typical
fish stores we came across a bucket full of eyes staring at us. These were big frogs
with only their eyes sticking out of the water.

amazing 66 is truly amazing

Frog and twin rice

When we inquired where in Chinatown we could find the best-prepared frogs, the answer was of course the Amazing 66. Both of us are adventurous diners and that way we discovered the phenomenal kitchen of this top restaurant.

Helen Ng, the very proud owner, loves traditional family-style Chinese food. The menu contains predominately Cantonese specialties. The diverse varieties of frog dishes are fabulous, the dry fried frog legs are coated with a superb batter and the frog stew with chestnuts is characterized by lovely fresh frog meat. One of the showpieces is the frog and twin rice. Twin rice is a balanced, diversified rice dish consisting of six different types, in this case prepared with frog parts in order to give it an extra punch of flavor. The perfect stir-fried vegetables and the more noble parts of the frog do the rest. Wow! The twin rice is truly one of the best rice dishes I have ever eaten. The taste, the crispness and the mouth-feel illustrate the professional skill of a great chef, who is moreover challenged by a lady who knows what she wants. The result is that he has really outdone himself.

The restaurant has far more selections than just frog dishes. I was knocked off my feet by the kabocha green pumpkins, prepared whole and filled with phenomenally seasoned and slow-cooked beef. All the dishes are nicely presented and very tasty. Feel free to ask Helen for advice in selecting your dishes. Amazing 66 is truly amazing. An address you will love.

DI PALO

200 Grand Street (@Mott Street) - NY 10013
T (212) 226-1033 - www.dipaloselects.com
Open Mon-Sat: 9:00 a.m. - 6:30 p.m., Sun: 9:00 a.m. - 4:00 p.m.

Di Palo is a conception far beyond Little Italy. The history of this neighborhood store
began in 1903 when Savino Di Palo decided to change the course of his life and emigrate
to the US, just like many other Italians.

Mozzarella

mozzarella doesn't get any better than this

This cheese maker from the small village of Montemilone in Basilicata left everything behind, including his family, friends and farm. He liked what he found in Little Italy and he opened a latteria (dairy bar) in 1910. When WWI broke out in 1914, the rest of his family joined him in NY and they decided to honor the traditions they brought from Basilicata.

Savino's daughter, Concetta, opened her own shop in 1925 on the corner of Mott and Grand, a half a block from her father's store where she sold a number of cheeses produced by her father and her husband Luigi. Two generations later, the brothers Salvatore (Sal to his friends) and Lou and their sister Marie decided to broaden the original 1903 mission of Savino. The current fifth generation is now importing top artisinal cheeses and fine cold cuts from their homeland. These are sold alongside their own cheese production, which includes caciocavallo, provolone, pecorino romano, and of course their top cheese: the best mozzarella in the world!

The word, "mozzarella" comes from the Italian verb *mozzare* (which means both "to cut" and "cut off"). For ages it has been produced in the southern part of Italy from rich buffalo milk. The term first appeared in 1570 in the cookbook of Bartolomeo Scappi.

Actually, I am not supposed to use the term mozzarella, because when mozzarella is made of cow's milk, the cheese is actually called fior di latte. In Di Palo, this is freshly made in front of you in the store; it can't be fresher than that. When I took a friendly Belgian restaurant owner, who often visits southern Italy and owns land there, around NY, I said to him: "You will now taste the best mozzarella ever." He laughed and told me that he goes to farms in Campania to taste mozzarella and buys the cheese there. How could this version of mozzarella from the center of NY come close to his? We eagerly tasted one of these mozzarellas that we bought at the doorstep of Di Palo. Although he never actually said it to me, from the look on his face I could just hear him think: "Damn, he is right." That is Di Palo for me: he makes something that everyone knows, yet makes it so well that everyone rediscovers it and asks himself why so much bad mozzarella is eaten. Di Palo is one of the NY businesses that I miss the most. I cannot thank Sal and Lou enough for their magisterial fior di latte.

GRAND/BOWERY STREET FOOD CART

Grand St./Bowery St. - NY 10013

Open for lunch and dinner

During the summer, I occasionally sit in the Sarah Roosevelt Park
to watch a soccer match.

Pigskin with radish

In NYC you will find plenty of fantastic basketball games played on all types of courts with hip-hop playing in the background, but watching a soccer match in a park is not so simple.

When I was a kid and went to soccer matches with my father and uncle, it was always inextricably bound up with eating a far too greasy, messy hamburger with tasteless onions on a tasteless bun. In NYC, going to watch soccer in the park goes hand in hand with eating fantastic, slowly cooked pigskin with large, juicy and tasty pieces of daikon (radish).

This sublime treat comes from a modest food cart a little further down on the corner of Grand and Bowery. The pleasant proprietor is also very helpful, which is just as well, because his menu is only in Chinese. The food he serves is genuinely homemade and once it is finished, there is no more. For me, the pigskin is a true topper, but many customers swear by his homemade fish balls. If I am in a real decadent mood, I ask for a combination of fish balls, pigskin and daikon. Then it is quite clear that we are not only talking about taste, but also about sublime textures.

CHEE CHEONG FUN FOOD CART

Elisabeth St./Hester St. - NY 10013

Open daily 7:00 a.m. - 7:00 p.m.

When the streets of NY are covered with snow that just keeps falling,
and you trudge your way through Chinatown, the sight of the steamy food cart,
half-covered by a tarp, is a relief, a sort of light at the end of the tunnel.

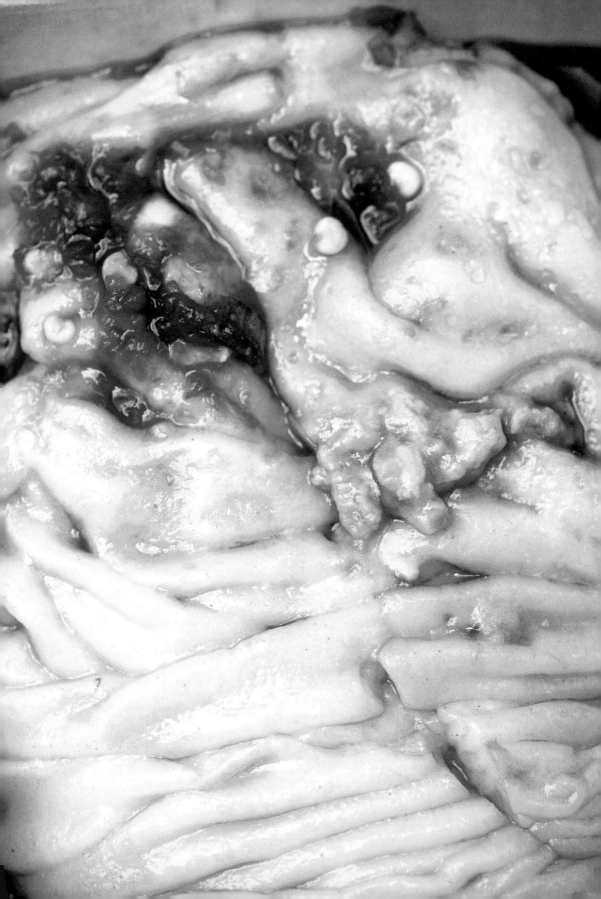

Chee cheong fun

cooking in the danger zone

This modest conveyance, which seems to come from one of the episodes of *Cooking in the Danger Zone* is operated by a very diminutive woman who is always up and about and is happy to conjure her hearty and tasty dishes. I call her Ah Yee, which means "small aunt". Her à la minute steamed chee cheong fun with fresh chives, pork or chicken, egg, some peanuts and soy sauce are ideal for breakfast, although I can eat it all day. Ah Yee works here from 7:00 a.m. to 7:00 p.m.

Chee cheong fun is a traditional dish from the dim sum culture of southern China and it means "noodles in the shape of a pig's large intestines." If you look at the shape, this is a well-chosen metaphor. Just like so many easy-to-prepare dishes, the subtle differ-ence in the handling and preparation makes all the difference. A measure of rice flour, 1/4 measure of tapioca flour mixed with the same quantity of water and the fundament of your cheong fun, your runner on base, as it were, is ready. The liquid mixture is then poured into a flat steam pot especially designed for the purpose and is slowly steamed into an extremely thin rice sheet. The thinner, the better and prettier the texture. The filling is added when the noodle is nearly done so that the mixture attaches itself further around the filling and sticks to it. The thin rice sheet is than folded into thirds and sprinkled with soy sauce. The chee cheong fun of Ah Yee has a texture that reveals great craftsmanship. To be honest, it doesn't have to snow for me to make a stop at her cart.

FUNG TU

22 Orchard St. (between Canal St. and Hester St.) - NY 10002
T (212) 219-8785 - www.fungtu.com
Open Tues-Sat: 6:00 p.m. - midnight, Sun: 4:00 p.m.-10:00 p.m.

Keep in mind the names Jason Wagner, John Wells and Jonathan Wu!
Together they make up Fung Tu, a hidden jewel located
where Chinatown actually begins.

East meets West

White asparagus,
hundred-year old egg,
dried doufu-ru
and Chinese chives

Here on the border of Chinatown and the Lower East Side, in the building where Fung Tu is now located, there was once a noodle factory. But this restaurant is intimate and modern and perfectly complements the style of the presentation and taste of the food.

Did Jane d'Arensbourg, the wife of Chef Wu, have a *cha chaan teng* in mind when she designed the interior of his intimate restaurant? A sort of old fashion Hong Kong coffee house that stood central in Wong Kar Wai's masterpiece, *In the Mood for Love*? In any case, the restaurant is full of tranquil elements that also characterize her husband's dishes.

Jonathan Wu cooked for a long time at Per Se and that explains his preference in his mature dishes for a delicate and fragile look. His partnership with Wilson Tang, the youngest scion of the Nom Wah Original Tea Parlor, is illustrated by the presence of the original egg roll "version 2." The cuisine of

the restaurant is a true dynamic, creative work in progress, gently evolving into its own form and style. The white asparagus is a fine example, cooked to al dente perfection and topped with lesser known seasoning, cut in the very precise brunoise manner, with the topping chopped up in tiny little cubes. The combination has a superb effect.

The theme of this book calls for a Must Eat selection, but this is a little disrespectful for the concept of this restaurant. The menu is an open invitation to discover a personal vision of the Chinese-American kitchen; in other words, the menu tells us a deeply personal Chinese-American tale. As soon as you step into this restaurant, you feel the necessity for detail and precision. A glance at the wine and beverage list compiled by Jason says enough: subtlety, *terroir* and purity are the mantras. Fung Tu offers a very fascinating and tasteful kitchen that is in perfect balance. East meets West in a mature and credible manner.

BLACK SEED BAGELS

170 Elisabeth St. (Kenmare and Spring St.) - NY 10012
www.blackseedbagels.com
Daily 7.00 a.m. - 4:00 p.m.

For me, the bagel is as inextricably bound up with NYC as the Statue of Liberty.
The bagel is nonetheless as old as the street.

Hand-rolled wood-fired oven poppy seed bagel, homemade cream cheese, beet-cured salmon, radish, herbs

The first time the word "bagel" came up was in 1610 in the municipal by-laws of Krakow, Poland. An interesting anecdote is that in Krakow, any woman who gave birth used to receive a gift of a bagel. The popularity of the bagel grew and in the 16th and 17th centuries it became a part of the daily diet of every Pole. Quite plausible is that the original word derives from *beugal* or *bügel*, due to the irregular shape of the handmade bagels. Bagels were brought to the US by Polish-Jewish immigrants and they quickly gained a strong foothold on these shores. The legendary Bagel Bakers Local 338, dating from the early part of the 20th century, was a tremendous success, creating pride in the craftsmanship required to produce handmade bagels. It was in 1960 that Harry Lender and his son Murray turned the bagel into a national craze when they automated bagel production and began to distribute frozen bagels.

That spelled the demise of the bagel as an artisanal product, but fortunately there were initiatives such as the Black Seed Bagel store. The bagels in this store are made from scratch and waiting in line here also provides a marvelous spectacle. Kate Burr and her team are amazingly motivated, even when the line gets unbearably long. You see all the phases of bagel production occur with precision and dedication, in front of your eyes. Organic flour, salt, water and yeast are kneaded into a hefty dough. The dough is then rolled out into longer sausages and subsequently into the typical ring with the hole-in-the-middle shape of a bagel. Before they are cooked in water, these bagel rings rise for at least 12 hours at 40-50 °F. Once they have cooled down, they are baked in a wood oven at a temperature of 400-570° F. Only respect for these traditional methods will get you a Platonic shiny bagel with the authentic proper texture on the inside.

Since the bagels are made especially for you, you can also choose your filling. The bagels can be filled with sophisticated combinations, resulting in a festive meal. Even while typing these words on my laptop, I can recall the irresistible aroma of fresh bagels. I am totally content whenever I sit on a small bench at the front of this tranquil part of Elisabeth Street while I see and smell the perfect bagel, filled with red beet, lox, homemade cream cheese, fresh radishes and herbs.

Bagels are so popular that on his 2008 Space Shuttle mission, NASA astronaut, Gregory Chamitoff, brought a gift of 18 sesame seed bagels to the astronauts at the International Space Station who had been circling the earth for far too long. Black Seed Bagels change your outlook on bagels forever.

CHIKALICIOUS DESSERT BAR

203 E. 10th St. (between 1st Avenue and 2nd Avenue) - NY 10009
T (212) 475-0929 - www.chikalicious.com
Thurs-Sun: 3:00 p.m. - 10:30 p.m.

There is hardly any type of food that you can't get in the Big Apple, but restaurants that only
serve desserts are rare. Here you find two alongside one other.

Fromage blanc island cheesecake

On one side of the street is the ChikaLicious Dessert Bar that serves complex restaurant desserts in the form of a brief tasting menu, and on the other side, the ChikaLicious Dessert Club with desserts that indeed come from the same kitchen but are sold more in a baking shop set-up. There is also a tiny eating area.

I met Don Tillman for the first time when he was practicing his other passion; he was playing his saxophone at the Union Square Market. His greatest sources of inspiration are John Coltrane, Miles Davis and Louis Armstrong, and also his wife Chika. With her, he ate at many places around the world and came to realize that good food is actually a type of edible memory.

Chika, who comes from Japan, has the focus of a top-class sushi maker as she works unperturbed on her desserts for the customers visiting this tiny niche restaurant. Just as you would expect, the open kitchen is the epitome of order and neatness. The place sits only twenty lucky souls. Her work is innovative; the motif is the 'unbearable lightness' of desserts. I recall that her doughssant – a spin-off of/homage to Dominique Ansel's Cronut – comes scrupulously close to the original in terms of the total experience.

NYC has a thing with cheesecake. Cheesecake was already baked by the ancient Greeks, served to Olympian athletes as early as 776 BCE. Marcus Cato, a Roman politician is credited with the first cheesecake recipe, recorded in the 1st century BCE. However, it was not until the discovery of cream cheese in 1872 and its further development by James Kraft in 1928, that the cheesecake in its current form became world-known. Chika looks at this from a Japanese perspective and makes a nearly feathery version without losing any of the taste. The lemon grass panna cotta, perfect in consistency, is coupled with a sorbet made of basil, mango and sweet basil seeds; a coconut marshmallow together with ginger shortbread and for chocoholics – an incredible adult chocolate pudding on double chocolate sable (shortbread biscuit). A lovely and original address to cherish. This is a place that must definitely be visited more than once.

DOWNTOWN EAST

ADDITIONAL EATERIES

 NARCISSA
21 Cooper Square - NY 10003
T +1 212 228 3344
www.narcissarestaurant.com
▸ Carrots Wellington

 CHERCHE MIDI (SHANE MCBRIDE)
282 Bowery - NY 10012
T +1 212 226 3055
www.cherchemidiny.com
▸ Homemade Lobster Ravioli in ginger beurre blanc
with piquillo peppers

 ESTELA
47 E Houston Street - NY 10012
T +1 212 219 7693
www.estelanyc.com
▸ Gnocchi

 GOLDEN CADILLAC
13 1st Avenue (corner of 1 Street & 1 Street) - NY 10003
T +1 212 995 5151
www.goldencadillacnyc.com
▸ Monte Christo minis with el Guapo tequila cocktail

 SUSHI DOJO
110 1st Avenue (7th Street) - NY 10009
T +1 646 692 9398
www.sushidojonyc.com
▸ Nama tako (Live octopus sushi)

MOMOFUKU NOODLE BAR
163 First Avenue (between 10th and 11th Street)
NY 10003
T +1 212 475 7899
www.momofuku.com/new-york/noodle-bar
▸ Pork belly bun

CHA AN TEA HOUSE
230 E 9th Street (between 2d & 3d) - NY 10003
T +1 212 228 8030
www.chaanteahouse.com
▸ Tea smoked salmon

GOLDEN UNICORN
18 East Broadway (tussen Catherine & Market Street) - NY
10002
T +1 212 941 0911
www.goldenunicornrestaurant.com
▸ Siu mai

 YUNNAN KITCHEN
79 Clinton Street - NY 10002
T +1 212 253 2527
www.yunnankitchen.com
▸ Spicy Cumin Chicken, charred okra,
long peppers, crispy rice

 LOMBARDI PIZZA
32 Spring Street (Mott & Mulberry) - NY 10012
T +1 212 941 7994
www.firstpizza.com
▸ Pizza Margharita

 MISSION CANTINA
172 Orchard Street (Stanton Street) - NY 10002
T +1 212 254 2233
www.missioncantinanyc.com
▸ Pork jowl, pig ear, pork shoulder

 GRAFFITI
224 East 10 Street (between 1st and 2d Avenue) - NY 10003
T +1 212 677 0695
www.graffitinyc.com
▸ Chickpea crusted skate, mint yoghurt sauce

 TORRISI
250 Mulberry Street (between Prince and Spring) - NY 10012
T +1 212 965 0955
www.torrisinyc.com
▸ 20 course tasting menu

GOTHAM BAR & GRILL
12 East 12th Street (between 5th Avenue and University Place)
NY 10003
T +1 212 620 4020
www.gothambarandgrill.com
▸ Niman Ranch Pork Chop 41
Braised greenmarket kale, poached apricots,
baby turnips, polenta, sage port wine reduction

 MILE END DELI
53 Bond Street - NY 10012
T +1 212 529 2990
www.mileenddeli.com
▸ Ruth Wilensky sandwich
(house made beef salami, onion roll, mustard)

SHOOLBRED'S
197 2nd Avenue - NY 10003
T +1 212 529 0340
www.shoolbreds.com
▸ Lamb sliders with mint chutney,
crumbled feta, whole weat potato roll

VALPO GATES
(718) 497-1450

ALPHABETICAL INDEX

Colophon

www.lannoo.com
Register on our website to regularly receive
our newsletter with new publications as well as exclusive offers.

Texts: Luc Hoornaert
Photography: Kris Vlegels
             Nomad@The Nomad Hotel © *Nomad* - Eleven Madison © *Francesco Tonelli*
             Buddakan © *Buddakan* - Nakazawa Sushi © *Daniel Krieger* - Babbo © *Melanie Dunea*
Graphic design: Grietje Uytdenhouwen & Peer bvba
Illustrations: Emma Thyssen
Cartography: Elke Feusels
Translation: Bracha De Man

If you have any questions or remarks, do not hesitate to contact our editorial team:
redactiekunstenstijl@lannoo.com.

© Lannoo Publishers, Tielt, 2014
2nd print run
ISBN: 978 94 014 1914 7
Registration of copyright: D/2014/45/336
NUR: 440